Heaven
SENT

EMMA BEAUCHESNE

ISBN 978-1-68197-868-0 (Paperback)
ISBN 978-1-68197-869-7 (Digital)

Christian Faith Publishing, Inc.
296 Chestnut Street
Meadville, PA 16335
www.christianfaithpublishing.com

Photo Credits:

Adventure-Bound Rafting
Holt International
Jack Beauchesne
Jason Beauchesne
Kurt Nezbeda
Sean Vaillancourt
Steven Vannest

Printed in the United States of America

PREFACE

I have never been one to talk much; maybe it is due to my mind constantly wandering into the deep mysteries of life. My brain cannot fully grasp the concepts of even simple things because they almost always lead back to a vast structure of something my mind is incapable of perceiving. Take a glass of water for example; most of my peers would likely take a sip of the liquid and not think of a mere thought as it cooled down their esophagus. I, on the other hand, would most likely zone out with my pupils dilated to full capacity in awe of the water inside. You see, millions of thoughts would come to my mind about the water alone, excluding the glass in which it is present. Where did the water come from? How is it that the water is so pure? These miniscule questions would then lead to something like, Were not we once pure like the water? Was not Jesus like the water all throughout His life, pure, incapable of even the slightest sin? The thoughts would then linger throughout my cranium until a fellow soul would be kind enough to point out that I have been staring at the glass of water for a generous five minutes and that I resemble a complete lunatic.

The truth is, I consider myself to be intelligent. I have received excellent grades. I was a participant in a spelling bee after winning the classroom bee; after creating a distinguished essay on my affection for the realm of science, I was granted a scholarship to a camp that excelling students would attend to study marine biology, and I was given the opportunity to take an advanced test to attend a Johns Hopkins camp after exceeding in a literary examination. Now that I have listed some of my achievements, I can proudly explain to you that none of them influenced my point of view on my intelligence whatsoever. The only reason I consider myself bright or beautiful or purposeful or anything for that matter is because of who created me. God creates all things with the intended purpose for them to be useful, amazing creations to display His glory throughout this temporary earth. God created us as intelligent, beautiful, prosperous creatures. He sees all of us the same, so I do consider myself wonderful, not because of who I am, but because of who God is and what He genuinely created me to be.

"God saw all that He had made, and it was very good." (Genesis 1:31 NIV)

Growing up, I did not always have this outlook on life. I used to be so caught up in my own flaws and sought after approval from everyone except God, which would get me nowhere except in my room with my back pressed up against a wall. Words were something I took so literally that I would obsess over and end up trying to change my appearance to compensate for them. I remember a girl calling me pretty in an obviously sarcastic tone. I do not remember seeing myself as pretty since then until this year. The saying "Sticks and stones may break my bones, but words will never hurt me" is a straight-up lie. Words are powerful and can do a ton of damage. Because of a single sentence, I was slowly fading and seeing myself as more worthless every single day.

"The words of the reckless pierce like swords, but the tongue of the wise will bring healing." (Proverbs 12:18 NIV)

The purpose of this manuscript is to give you a glimpse of how much the creator of this world loves you. My stories are intended to be an example of what God did through my life, and I pray that God works through yours as well.

God bless.

CHAPTER ONE

Love

I often catch myself seeking approval of others and drift off into my own delusional location where all I care about is that exact concept. It is like I am trying to fill a void with love even though I am not quite sure what the definition of love exactly is. The standard definition of love is "an intense feeling of deep affection." But this brings me to the conclusion that we all create our own standards about what love truly is. It takes our own definition of "deep affection" to decide whether we love something or not. I was pondering this thought and began to look into it.

Recently, I was listening to a sermon that my pastor was delivering this past Thursday. The message was based on the utter fact that God is purely incapable of speaking even the tiniest lie. He mentioned that since we are aware of this, God's word is holy and valid. This brings me back to my original thought. If we want a true definition of what love truly is, we should automatically refer to scriptures. Even in the very beginning of the Bible, God talks about this "love" and says many different things about what it is. After going through many passages about love, here is my favorite definition:

"Love is patient, love is kind. It does not envy, it does not boast, it is not proud. It does not dishonor others, it is not self-seeking, it is not easily angered, it keeps no record of wrongs." (1 Corinthians 13:4–5 NIV)

I believe that God creates a crystal-clear image on how we should be loving others in these very brief verses. After all, Jesus lived the most loving life out of any human to live, so we can also refer to His life as an example of how to love everyone. I even wrote a song about these verses! It goes like this:

You are patient
You are kind
You do not envy at any time
You're not proud
You do not boast
You love others the very most
What is love
What is love
What is love that never fails
You don't dishonor
Your sons and daughters
You don't get mad
With the truth you're glad
You forgive
Don't delight in evil
But rejoice for the truth of the people
You love us all
You died to take away it all
You died in pain
To take away our shame
That is love
That is love
That is love that never fails
You protect
And you trust

You made us breathe out of the dust
You have hope
You persevere
God we know you're always near
What is love
What is love
What is love that never fails
And in our broken and crumbling souls
We know your love can guide us home
And when we've wandered and lost our way
You'll bring us back so we can say
You love us all
You died to take away it all
You died in pain
To take away our shame
That is love
That is love
That is love that never fails
God is love
God is love
God is love that never fails
You are love that never fails

The cross is an upright, bold symbol of love. It displays the love that Christ passed on to us after He took the weight of the world upon His very own shoulders, drank our sin, sacrificed Himself, and forgave us. Christ is love.

"We love because He first loved us." (1 John 4:19 NIV)

Before Jesus sacrificed Himself, there was not a human example of love. Now, we are capable of experiencing love by accepting the sacrifice that Jesus laid out for us. After grasping the amount of love that was embodied for us, we can ask God to help us apply that to our lives we live today. When we are filled up by love, we can use it as a way to radiate God's glory to people around us so that they might experience the same type of phenomenon that we have been gifted.

Sometimes, we are quick to say we love something, but I think that it is vital that we understand what we are saying. If we say that we love everything without thinking about what it means, love turns into a bland word that inevitably holds no value. If we use God's definition of love to determine whether we love something, we can actually be accurate with our judgments. I use this same method with any relationship I have with friends, family, and others whom I'm close to. If you replace the word "love" in First Corinthians 13:4–5 with who (or what) you are determining your love for, you can see if you really do in fact love that particular person (or thing). For example,

_____ is patient, _____ is kind, _____ does not envy, _____ does not boast, _____ is not proud, _____ does not dishonor others, _____ is not self-seeking, _____ is not easily angered, _____ keeps no record of wrongs.

I hope that this technique guides you to seek healthy, Jesus-centered relationships with others. If we break down this verse, we can paint an even more vivid picture of how to love others by our actions and words.

"Love is patient."

The first key to living out love is patience. Patience is one of the fruits of the spirit (Galatians 5:22), and it shows up multiple times in the Bible. So what exactly is patience? I believe that patience, in a way, is trusting God.

We are not meant to do everything all at once; sometimes we need to put in effort and persevere to accomplish tasks. If we get overwhelmed, we are sometimes quick to quit or end soon. If we are patient, we can trust God to work amazing opportunities into our lives and develop even more patience for later on. It can be hard to wait for things sometimes, but if we are trusting God's will, the outcome will be worth the wait.

An example of patience brings me back to fifth grade. I was a small blond kid with braces and a slowly developing faith. I longed to sing whenever I was offered the chance, and part of my worship time alone with God involved singing to every Christian song that was available to me. I would also pray a prayer something like this every night before I went to sleep:

"God, I know that you're there, but sometimes it's hard for me to feel your presence. But with every song that I sing, I mean every word with my heart and soul. It would be amazing if I could share this with other people if it is according to your will."

For a while, nothing happened, but I would still continue to pray that prayer every night. Several years had passed, and eighth grade began. I had been praying that prayer for four years, and soon it would come into play.

I went to the Dominican Republic for a mission trip in the eighth-grade, and it was halfway into the trip when I was dismissed for journaling time. (This is a picture of me with a few kids from the Dominican.)

I prayed one of the most real prayers that I ever had with God that day, and I also engaged in many life-changing interactions with others on my mission team and the locals from the villages that we visited. That day was the day I believe I fully accepted Jesus as my Lord and Savior. The next morning, I was scheduled to present my devotional that I had created for my team. Our group leader pulled me aside about five minutes before I began and informed me that I had received an e-mail from someone that worked at my school. I had only previously had a few wonderful exchanges with this lady before receiving this e-mail, so I was sure that she was unaware of the prayer that I had been praying every night. When I opened the e-mail, I was trying with all my effort not to cry because I was in so much awe of how God connected her to me. This is the e-mail:

> Hello, Emma,
>
> I pray that this letter finds you well and that you are enjoying your trip. I know when my daughters went to the Dominican, they came back changed in many ways. I know that the Lord opened up their eyes to many things and birthed a compassion in them for his children. My oldest daughter, Rachel, ended up going back three times because she loved it so much.
>
> Well, the reason that I'm writing is because about two weeks ago (maybe a little longer), I had a dream about you. The Lord sometimes speaks to me in my dreams. It was very simple... simply "Emma can sing, and she has an amazing range, but she is very shy about it."
>
> Why would He drop that into my spirit? I think it was to get a message to you. Sometimes we have dreams in our heart, and we kind of ponder them and wonder if they will ever come to pass. I think the Lord wants you to know that He put that in you for a reason and not to be shy about it. The Word says,

"Delight yourself also in the Lord, and He shall give you the desires of your heart." (Ps. 37:4)

One way to take that is that if we delight in Him, He will give us our heart's desires—fulfill our desires. But another way to take it would be, He actually *gives* us our desires. In other words, it is *He* who put it in your heart to want to sing. He gave you that desire.

Whatever God gives us, He wants us to use. And whatever He commissions us for, He equips us for. He never leaves us without or in lack. He is Jehovah Jireh, the God that always provides.

Believe that the Lord has given you this gift for a purpose. You have a song to sing for Him, and it will be a blessing to many and bring deliverance. Open up to the Lord and just say, "Yes, Lord, whatever You want to do, I'm here," and together, you will be on a new wonderful adventure. You don't have to make things happen, and you don't have to work things out. The Lord will do that for you. He will move you forward, and you won't have to worry about getting people's attention with what He has given you. He'll do that for you. And when a door opens for you, know that you can go ahead and walk through because He is leading the way and He absolutely will not leave you hanging. His grace and favor are upon you, and He will be faithful to you with His love.

The blessing of the Lord is upon you, Emma! May He continue to work in you and bring you closer to Him on this trip and always! Have a great time!

Sincerely,

Mrs. Seward (the office lady! ha ha!)

That e-mail was the exact thing that I needed as validation to understand that God had been there 24-7 and that He can help in ways we would not even think of. After that single prayer, I received that e-mail. After that e-mail, I sang for my family. After singing to my family, I sang in front of my school. After singing in front of my school, I posted some cover videos, and now I sing almost every week in front of my entire high school during chapel time. God is opening up so many unique opportunities for me, and I am always excited to see how He writes another chapter in my life.

This is why we should be patient. If I had given up on praying that prayer to God, who knows? Maybe I would still be the same anxiety-ridden shy girl that I used to be in the fifth grade. If we are patient in God, we can have more opportunities and be closer to understanding the true definition of love.

The next part of the verse is kindness. Kindness is also one of the fruits of the spirit and is something that can be really exciting. My favorite way to show kindness is to do random things for others to show them that I care about them. There are so many options available, and the possibilities are endless. Kindness can really be any-thing to share the love that we have been given with others. I recently watched a video of these people from a church organization who prayed with a homeless woman and then supported her financially. When a random act of kindness is offered, people may be more open to receiving prayer and finding more information regarding Jesus. If you would like to check it out, it can be found at:

https://www.youtube.com/watch?v=FP7d7NT5wyI

The third part of the verse is about not becoming jealous. God makes it clear that we should not eyeball possessions that were not meant for us.

The Ten Commandments include this same statement, and we should know that it is an important commandment. Now that I have more knowledge, I do not understand the need for jealousy. If God loves each and every one of us on the exact same level, what are we actually jealous of? God made us all unique and made us the way we are for different reasons. Even if we needed to be jealous, why would we be jealous of materialistic items, body types, or anything else if we are going to leave all of it in the future? Shouldn't we be focusing on our relationship with our savior instead of trying to impress people who are on the same level as us from God's point of view?

I think that the next two points fit well together. Being prideful and boasting about our accomplishments are not intended to be on our agenda. Like I said, God sees all of us the same, so there is no need to flaunt our achievements or money around like we run the world. The Bible talks about God opposing the proud yet loving the humble. Jesus did this very thing by not putting Himself on a higher level and hung around with the sinners, humbling Himself. Jesus humbled Himself so much that He healed leprosy by touching the infected skin and He talked and dined with those whom everyone around Him thought to be a disgrace to the community.

Jesus also did not dishonor others. He never made someone feel lower than Himself. One of my favorite passages tells about a woman pouring expensive perfume on the feet of Jesus and wiping His feet with tears and her hair. She humbled herself and loved Jesus more than the others who were considered honored by the surrounding people in the community.

The honored men, however, sought attention and decided to treat the woman as less than who she was while Jesus lifted her spirits and forgave her sins. Jesus did not dishonor the humbled woman but opposed the proud men who were bashing the woman's reputation.

Narcissistic thinking is not something that the Lord chooses to take favor in. Love is an amazing thing, but it can be used incorrectly if we choose to point too much of it toward ourselves. We were made to love others around us instead of keeping it all to ourselves. This also goes along the lines with being prideful because if we hold ourselves at a higher standard than anyone else, our peers will most likely take offense to it. Take King Nebuchadnezzar for example. He thought that he was the ruler of everything until he had his dream interpreted by Daniel and chose to finally surrender "his" kingdom to God. As humans, we enjoy building our own kingdoms, but those kingdoms might end up crashing down on us, so we should choose to give them up and start building the eternal kingdom that we know will never fall, which is heaven.

"Love is not easily angered."

I know someone extremely close to me who used to have a relationship like this. The other person in the relationship was very ill-tempered, and when they were mad, things escalated quickly. Luckily, their relationship ended because it turned out to be unhealthy. After hearing about this, the person telling me this story told me that they always felt some regret about hurting the person with whom the relationship ended, even after many years had passed. I wanted them to know and anyone going through something similar that love is not supposed to involve easily angered partners because God has something else spectacular in mind.

The final aspect of love is being able to forgive. This aspect is very basic and all primarily comes down to this: Jesus died for all our sins and knew the wages of every one of them, so forgiving should be something we all should do since we have also been forgiven of our trespasses.

I heard a story from a friend about a reckless driver who killed several passengers in a collision. The mother of the victims eventually forgave the driver but took some harsh ridicule for doing so. Many would argue that they would never forgive anyone who killed their children, but I think that this was a wonderful example of a woman not only living out her faith by words but by actions and, most importantly, love. She was able to forgive the driver after realizing that her burden was lifted off her back for her sins paid in full, so it was only fair to forgive the driver since Jesus had died for her own sins.

So now we have a biblically determined definition of love, and we know how we can share it with others. We are patient to let God work in our lives; we are kind to others. Jealousy is unnecessary to us; we don't become prideful or self-seeking. We humble ourselves, we are not angered easily, and we forgive everything. If we act like this, others might understand how to love and what it truly is. We know that Jesus was the perfect example of love, so let's look at how He loved and continues to do so.

Jesus was sent to the earth by God, His Father. He was the only son that God had, and He was born by virgin birth. God loved Jesus so much, but something deceitful happened on the earth. Sin was everywhere, and there was not a single human without sin except for Jesus. God was very upset because He knew the fate of Jesus. Someone had to die, as the wages of sin are death, and the options were either everyone would have to die or the only human to ever live a pure life would. Jesus was eating His final meal with His disciples and He knew that He would soon be brutally murdered by the Roman guards under Pontius Pilate. He spent some time praying in Gethsemane where He was so frightened that He sweat out blood (hematidrosis). He was as much of a human as we are. He felt pain, He had feelings, He walked in fear, and He was inordinately capable of love. When Jesus was arrested, He was able to leave at any moment by denying that He was the son of God, but He did not. He stood His ground and suffered a horrible death on the cross after He was scourged forty times with whips made with lead ends and sheep bones tied to leather. They spat on Him and hit Him with a wooden staff and made Him carry His own cross up a hill. Nails pierced through His skin in between His radius and His ulna, and His feet were bound and pierced with nails as well. Jesus breathed His last breath on the cross and then died. The Romans pierced His side with a spear to make sure He was dead. Jesus died out of love to take away all our sins.

"But He was pierced for our transgressions, He was crushed for our iniquities; the punishment that brought us peace was on Him, and by His wounds we are healed." (Isaiah 53:5 NIV)

This is what the ultimate example of love looks like. A man went through so much pain, all because He cared about each and every one of us with everything that He had.

The story of Jesus thankfully does not end there. After Jesus died, the guards placed Jesus in a tomb and sealed it off with a boulder covering the entrance. Three days after Jesus died, He rose from the dead. There was a shroud covering the face of Jesus when He was entombed, and scientists were trying to determine if they had uncovered an image directly from the face of Jesus. There were carbon-dating tests done on the Shroud of Turin, and the scientists concluded that it was not valid. There were two Christians who believed that it was valid. They questioned the scientists where they took the sample from to do carbon dating. All from two bystanders, the scientists were proved wrong after they noticed that the sample that they took from the shroud was actually a repaired patch, which would make their test extremely inaccurate. If you love scientific evidence like I do, you'll want to investigate some more here:

https://www.youtube.com/watch?v=0FRU92fJO_g

The first person to see Jesus was Mary. Jesus showed the marks that the nails had left in His flesh and told everyone that there would now be hope. God forgave the sins on earth because His son had died for them.

We know that we can be forgiven now and will never be separated from God because of the love that Jesus gave to us out of shedding His blood. If you want to accept the love that has been given to us, you can pray a prayer like this:

"Jesus, I know that you died a horrible death for me on the cross. You suffered and were as human as I am. Because of your love, the true love, I am here today. I repent from my sins and ask for your forgiveness. I accept the love that you gave to me when you died that day. In your holy and precious name I pray. Amen."

If you just prayed this prayer, you have just let Jesus intervene in your life and allowed Him to start working in you. You can experience His true love and love others while you come to know how your Savior loves you.

Now let's talk about how God the Father loves us. We know that Jesus was the flesh form of God and that He died because He loves us so much. God loves us so much that He gave up His precious son to die a gruesome death on a rugged cross. He knew what Jesus would have to go through and had to make the decision to sacrifice Him so that we could all be free.

"For God so loved the world that He gave His one and only son, that whoever believes in Him shall not perish but have eternal life." (John 3:16 NIV)

This verse is probably the most known Bible verse in scriptures, but have you ever thought about why that is? This single verse explains the majority of the Bible. It explains that our God loved us so much, that He allowed His one and only son to be crucified. His son wept for us while He was slowly dying, not because He was in unbearable pain, but because He looked down on the corrupt world that His Father had built. There was so much detail and many beautiful things, but sin got in the way of it all and destroyed the world.

Love is the initial concept that we need to know. As babies, we had to rely on love from our parents because we were not able to take care of ourselves. The same thing is true to this very day. We are all broken people, and we need God to take care of us and provide. Without God, nothing would exist. Without God, the world would be even more chaotic, and there would be no chance of hope to save us. God is love; He created it and shows us every day that He is Lord and that He loves all of us.

Sometimes when we are down in the dumps, we forget to look for the love that God has given us. He gives us the sunsets, the sunrises, the blue sky and clouds, the magnificent sun, the intricate solar system, and everything around us. God's love is everywhere, but it's up to us to choose whether we see it or not. As easy as it is for us to see love, it's also easy for us to see violence and hatred. If we put God in the limelight and make Him the focal point, there is no room for the violence and hatred to seep in.

We also may feel like God doesn't understand what we are going through. We assume that God is somewhere far away, but in reality, He meets us wherever we are and does not leave us.

The final part of the Trinity is the Holy Spirit, yet another way God shows His amazing love toward us. He sends His Spirit upon us so that we may attain a sense of peace, knowledge, and comfort in knowing that He is with us. The Spirit of God is always present, and we can be confident of that.

"And I will ask the father, and He will give you another advocate to help you and be with you forever." (John 14:16 NIV)

There are many other verses like this that indicate that God will send His Holy Spirit upon us when we ask.

Love is an amazing thing that anyone can experience. I once heard someone say, "Love is a universal language." It is so true. In every country I have visited, the languages differ, but there is always the language of love.

On the mission trip I went on, a little girl named Maura took my hand and smiled at me. I hadn't met her before, but I felt like we had known each other forever. Prior to the trip, I had a fear of the language barrier, but I soon realized that love can be displayed by so many things and not necessarily words. God wants us to love each other and makes it so simple for us to do so. It amazes me to see how many words there are for love:

English: love, German: liebe, Malay: suka, Thai: รัก, Afrikaans: lief, Greek: αγάπη, Malayalam: സ്നേഹം, Turkish: aşk, Albanian: Dashuri, Gujarati: પ્રેમ, Maltese: imħabba, Ukrainian: любов, Arabic: بالحب, Haitian: renmen, Maori: aroha, Vietnamese: yêu, Armenian: սիրել, Hausa: son, Marathi: i;iोम, Welsh: Caru, Azerbaijani: sevgi, Hebrew: בהוא, Mongolian: хайртай, Yiddish: עביל, Basque: maite, Hindi: प्यार, Nepali: i;iोम, Yoruba: ife, Belarusian: каханне, Hmong: hlub, Norwegian: elsker, Zulu: athande, Bengali: ভালবাসা, Hungarian: szerelem, Nyanja: kukonda, Bosnian: ljubav, Icelandic: elska, Persian: عشق, Bulgarian: обичам, Igbo: n'anya, Polish: miłość, Burmese: အချစ် [အ :ဂ၀ဝ၀ 0, Indonesian: cinta, Punjabi: ਪਿਆਰ ਦ ਜ, Catalan: amor, Irish: grá, Romanian: dragoste, Cebuano: paghigugma, Italian: amare, Russian: любовь, Chinese: 爱/愛, Japanese: 愛, Serbian: љубав, Croatian: ljubav, Javanese: tresna, Sinhala: ආදරය, Czech: milovat, Kannada:

;0_◌ℓ, Slovak: milovat', Danish: kærlighed, Kazakh: махаббат, Slovenian: Ljubezen, Dutch: liefde, Khmer: ful៣, Somali: jeclahay, Estonian: armastus, Korean: 사랑, Sudanese: bogoh, Filipino: pag-ibig, Lao: ຮັກ, Swahili: upendo, Finnish: rakkaus, Latvian: mīlestība, Swedish: älskar, French: amour, Lithuanian: meilė, Tajik: дӯст доштан, Galician: ame, Macedonian: сакам, Tamil: அ6ITL, Georgian: მიყვარს, Malagasy: fitiavana, Telugu: c0,;.._మ

Those are only some of the languages, but they all translate to one word which is love. This means that in every culture, there is love. God sent His son to die for the entire world, not just one part of it. It's mind-boggling to think about all the countries in the world and how God is working in them. Looking at all the countries' languages reminds me of the Tower of Babel. The Tower of Babel was built at a place where no one wanted to be split up after God instructed them to do so. God ended up confusing the people by giving them all different languages so that they had no choice but to split up. They called it Babel, and all their speech became "babbled" and misunderstood, if you will. It took awhile, but after realizing that they could not communicate with words, the people figured out that they could communicate not only by actions but love.

My family and I sponsor several children. We used to sponsor a girl named Nakshtra from India, and eventually she was adopted. After Nakshtra, we began sponsoring a different girl from India named Bujishree. Lastly, after I went to the Dominican Republic, my church had an event where we were able to experience poverty in a simulated tour without having to leave the country. I had already experienced it from actually leaving the country, but my parents and brother were able to experience it for the first time. After we did the experience, we decided as a family to sponsor a little boy from the Dominican Republic named Javiel. He is such a cutie! Today we received a letter from him with an adorable drawing. My point is, you can always share love with anyone even if they are many miles away from you. I think of the kids we sponsor as my siblings because we are all brothers and sisters in Christ and it's such a joy to love each other. If you're curious about the impact you could make in sponsoring a child, here is a link with more information and a picture of one of my sponsor sisters; Bujjishree.

https://holtsponsor.org:4443/sponsor/holt.writepage?page=photolisting5

God desires love in this world. He sacrificed so much for us because He, His son, and His Holy Spirit love us so much. As Christians, our purpose is to love one another and to share the good news that God has given us.

God wants us to love Him back. The most important one to love is God. God deserves every drop of love in us, and we should reflect His love to others around us. An amazing verse that goes along with this is

"Love the Lord your God with all your heart and with all your soul and with all your mind and with all your strength." (Mark 12:30 NIV)

Chapter 1 Reflection

- Have you accepted God's love?
- How can you share the love that God has given to you?
- What technique do you use to know if you love something?
- When was a time that you experienced love from God?

JOURNALING AND PRAYERS

CHAPTER TWO

Laminin

In science class this previous year, my teacher played an intriguing video for the class. The video began with a man preaching about a protein called laminin. The congregation was a bit confused because they had not known what Laminin was. Apparently, the preacher had run into a molecular biologist who told him about this protein. He explained that laminin held our bodies together and is in a very specific shape. He did not tell him the shape it was because he wanted the preacher to see it for himself. When the preacher searched "laminin" online, he was amazed at what he saw.

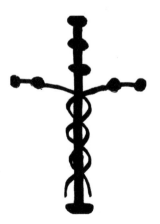

Laminin is in the shape of a cross. As Christians, the cross is a symbol of Jesus holding us together after He died for us. The fact that there is a protein that holds us together and is shaped like a cross is absolutely remarkable.

God glues our lives together and created our intricate bodies and the way that they function. It amazes me to know that God put this tiny protein in our bodies for us to find and know that it was placed there for a purpose. Could laminin be proof from God that He is holding us together? I think so.

Some of us want cold, hard evidence that God exists, and we rely on science to provide for this. Although I believe that we should not need this clarity to confess that God is above all, I think that science can be very interesting as it begins to study Christian beliefs. In this chapter, I will be talking about some of the phenomenons that science cannot explain and biblical proof that lines up with scientific information. In the meantime, you need to see this video on laminin. It's so cool.

https://www.youtube.com/watch?v=F0-NPPIeeRk

Let's go to the very beginning. It was controversial from the start.

Some scientists claim that the earth began with a "big bang." To go against this, some Christians say that God created the earth; therefore a "big bang" did not occur. But what if both of these statements somehow fit together, revealing the truth? Here is a possible theory:

"In the beginning, God created the heavens and the earth." (Genesis 1:1 NIV)

This is valid information; however, God also said, "Let there be light," and there was light. So if we connect these two and pair it with science, there is a possibility that God created a "big bang" of some sort. The past year, there was a study put out that revealed evidence about ripples in the space-time fabric of the universe. Some went as far as saying that it pointed back to the big bang theory. There was evidence that went along with it that suggested that the earth had a beginning. If we refer back to scriptures, this sounds very similar to the first verse written. This is good news to believers because it can aid in scientific support that the universe was made by a being outside of and not reliant on our universe. An ex-atheist saw the big bang as anything but a large explosion but as an extremely ordered event that by no chance could have randomly occurred.

When we look at science as Christians, some of us might feel like parts of it are secular. If we begin to think optimistically, we can understand that science is all about God! God created everything, and we are capable of researching His design through science. There is a movie called *God's Not Dead* in which a college professor challenges his student to a debate about whether or not God is real. In this movie, the first debate sums up a lot about what I am saying. The argument begins with the student explaining that atheists cannot disprove God. He talks about how the Bible lined up with many atheist scientists who had no bias. The student stood up for his faith when everyone was against him, and God gave him strength to accomplish his goal even in the face of negativity from his peers. I think that it would benefit all of us if we were to do the same. If we call ourselves Christians, we should be able to have evidence that we have studied God's creation. God wants us to research His creation because He made it for us to do so.

"Get wisdom, get understanding; do not forget my words or turn away from them." (Proverbs 4:5 NIV)

Have you ever looked at nature and been amazed by the intricacy of it all? Some of my greatest memories involved stargazing with my friends at camp. I would look up at the stars and feel so small from the knowledge I had about space. We are on a small planet in a galaxy among so many other galaxies, and God decided to put detail in even the tiniest objects in nature. I thought back to when God was telling Abraham that his descendants will be more numerous than the stars—the same stars that we see in the canopy of darkness in the sky. At the same camp, we watched a short film about God's creation in nature. My friend had a fear of lightning and was very frightened prior to the film because a storm was taking place. Once the film began, we knew that it was a message from God. A man described the way that things that scare us can be beautiful if we look at them with a different perspective. You might like it.

https://www.youtube.com/watch?v=loFBGdeXGtg

On the way back to our cabins that night, my friends and I stood in amazement at the beautiful streaks of light striking down. It changed from something dangerous to something magnificent. We can become stressed and overwhelmed if we are in a storm both figuratively and literally. One thing to keep in mind is that nature follows God.

"The men were amazed and asked, "What kind of man is this? Even the winds and the waves obey Him!" (Matthew 8:27 NIV)

We know that nature can never fail us in maintaining closeness with God because God created it. "Study nature, love nature, stay close to nature. It will never fail you." is a quote attributed to Frank Lloyd Wright. I always feel closer to God when I'm near a form of nature. It's nice to visibly see something that God created directly. This evening, I decided to go outside because I had not been out in a while. While I was outside, I stared at our bare fence that until recently was next to trees and wild plants. The trees were taken down to make room for a parking lot on the other side of the fence. However, there was one tree that had been left up. I stared at the tree for a couple minutes with my mind drifting off now and then. I wondered about how many others had been where I was sitting, staring at that exact tree. I wondered how old it was, if anything interesting once happened near it, or if it would soon be cut down. Then I looked at the stars and thought about the same thing. I wondered if generations before me had seen those exact stars or if a different human in a different location was looking at the sky at the same time as me.

One of my favorite songs by someone I was fortunate enough to meet, Jonathan Thulin, says, "There are a thousand trees blowing in the wind, witnesses to lives already lived."

These are such neat lyrics! They remind me that God created something as simple as a tree that stands tall in every season and is there through generation after generation. The chorus of the same song is this:

"Here I stand, here I stand on what you built, you are surrounding me, and the walls will never, ever, ever come down. You build me up like a city of gold, the battles rage, but I'm standing tall, you formed my heart like an empire, the wind and rain can't stop this fire. If only I could see it from your perspective, the beauty and the grace of your architecture."

"Architecture" by Jonathan Thulin,

https://itunes.apple.com/us/artist/jonathan-thulin/id302178847

The picture is of Jonathan Thulin and I.

We live in this beautiful piece of architecture that our creator has built for our lives. Nature is able to withstand rain, wind, snow, hail—whatever the storm may be—and we should be this way in our faith. No matter what life throws at us, God will always equip us with what we need to get through it all. After all, God put detail into flowers that will wither away and weeds that can become a nuisance, so imagine how much detail God put into each one of us and our lives.

Knowing that God created all of this earth, I have a longing to explore it. When I left the country for the first time, it broadened my horizons in the way that I knew that there was so much on this planet. I also discovered that there was more than land. I experienced many plane rides, looking down on the earth from a whole new perspective, and I earned my scuba diving license. I experienced the ocean in an entirely new way, interacting with foreign creatures that were absolutely breathtaking. It felt like a completely new world each time I would go below the surface. It also brought me to the realization that not everyone was able to experience this. There was a different world inside of ours that not many people had seen. There is beauty in a vast amount of places, but we need to travel to experience it. If we think about it, that is similar to life. We go through a long journey, traveling through obstacles until we finally meet our maker face-to-face. Even though the journey may seem difficult, God will send His spirit to guide us as we face trials of our faith and hardships.

"By day the Lord went ahead of them in a pillar of cloud to guide them on their way and by night in a pillar of fire to give them light, so that they could travel by day or night." (Exodus 13:21 NIV)

Dreams are a phenomenon that I seem to take an interest in. This is such a cool concept for Christians because dreams go back all the way to biblical times. God gave dreams to people as a way of communication. An example of this goes back to when King Nebuchadnezzar had his dream interpreted. He threatened to kill his servants if they didn't provide interpretation, but even with the circumstances, no one was able to interpret the dream until Daniel asked God to help him interpret the dream. Dreams are a small glimpse of how God communicates, and it is amazing to see the many ways He talks to His people.

Now that we studied some of the science that influences our modern-day lives, let's go back to the scriptures. There are small parts of scripture that indicate things to come before science was aware of it. Here are a few examples:

"What is the way to the abode of light? And where does darkness reside?" (Job 38:19 NIV)

In several translations of this verse, it mentions "the way," referring to light. In modern science, we have only recently discovered that light in fact has "a way." "The way," more specifically known as "electromagnetic radiation," traveling at around 186,000 miles per second. A different example of biblical evidence is found in this verse:

"The wind blows south and turns to the north; round and round it goes, ever returning on its course." (Ecclesiastes 1:6 NIV)

Here we have Solomon describing a type of cycle of air. Two thousand years later, scientists caught up and discovered the cycles for themselves. This next example is one of the most interesting discoveries that I have come across. There are five terms that science uses to express the universe: *time, space, matter, power*, and *motion*. In the first two verses of the Bible, this is validated.

"In the beginning, God created the heavens and the earth... and the spirit of God moved upon the face of the waters." (Genesis 1:1, 2 NIV)

Let's break this down:
- *"In the beginning."* Already, this refers to the first way that science uses to describe the universe, time.
- *"God created."* Now, there is yet another way that science uses to describe the universe, power.
- *"The heavens."* Here, we see the use of space, which is also in the description that science uses for the universe.
- *"And the earth."* We also see matter in the scriptures.

- *"And the spirit of God moved."* Lastly, we see motion take its place in scripture, completing every aspect that science used to describe the universe: time, space, matter, power, and motion.

A different example is as simple as a rainbow. It leads back to the story of Noah. God had destroyed everything on the earth with the breath of life in it except for Noah, his family, and two of every animal. After destroying the land and everything in it, God made a promise to Noah that He would never demolish the planet again. God declared a covenant with Noah and placed a rainbow in the sky so that Noah could remember this covenant always.

These are just some of the examples where scriptures line up with science. I think that some people want to be against a particular side, even though they do not contradict each other, so it is important to examine the evidence that the Bible gives us before we make false assumptions.

In my research, I came across a video that explained how science is accurate with biblical principles. The man in the video was explaining how the universe was capable of being created out of nothing with quantum fluctuations (laws of nature). When the set of forces are present, they are not physical, they can act on the physical, they create the physical from nothing, and they predate the universe. If we replace what we were defining with God, the Bible depicts this perfectly

https://www.youtube.com/watch?v=eQVm8RokoBA

I also came across another brilliant video that explained many discrepancies that scientists thought were in the Bible. The man speaking had a perspective that explained why some scientists are so opposed to there being a God. He said that it's not that they don't want there to be a God; it's most likely because they do not want a personal God.

https://www.youtube.com/watch?v=nEkWz6DAAOU

As time goes by, there is more and more scientific evidence that goes along with scriptures pertaining to the universe, weather, the atmosphere, and so many other concepts. The Bible has predicted what scientific evidence is only beginning to discover. The Bible holds information that science does not understand currently, but as time goes on, science may discover even more evidence that was already present in the Bible.

God created our lives for a purpose: to spread His love to everyone and to build His eternal kingdom. There is an extremely narrow part of time that earth can sustain life, and we are blessed enough to be born into that miniscule piece of time. Knowing this, we should understand that we are very important to God. He chose us as the few people to have the breath of life in us and to deliver His mission. We were not meant to go through life surviving, barely hanging on. We were meant to thrive and to seek the love that Jesus gave us and share it with everyone we possibly can before our earthly existence comes to an end.

Studying the Bible can give us a vast amount of insight of God's intended purpose for us, but even if we study everything in the Bible, it isn't necessarily going to do us any good if we don't take it to heart. You can be the most intelligent human in the realm of everything, but it won't mean anything if you are hypocritical and don't live out what you learn. Calling yourself a Christian does not mean that you know everything about Christianity. Being a Christian means that you want to understand God's word, and you live out what you learn and share it with others.

Chapter 2 Reflection

- Why is it important to look at the scriptures?
- What are some examples of revealed science in the Bible?
- Why is it good that there is evidence in the Bible that goes along with science?
- How can you use science to know that God has a purpose for your life?

JOURNALING AND PRAYERS

CHAPTER THREE

The Mountains

A s I have mentioned, I have always been fond of Christian music. (That's me singing at my eighth-grade graduation.)

Growing older and as the years slowly passed by me, I began to lose touch with mainstream music. I did not know why I lost interest in such music until I completely turned away from it. I am not saying that it is mandatory to do this, but in my circumstance, I believe that it complemented my walk with God. I realized that I could relate to Christian music and not so much with the mainstream choices. Whenever I read the word, the verses suddenly jump to songs that I have heard. Most Christian songs revolve around passages from the scriptures, so it's God's word firsthand. After not listening to secular music for a while now, I have lost interest in everything other than songs by Christian artists. More often than not, in the secular realm, I will hear lyrics bashing a certain group of people or complaining about a first-world problem. When I listen to Christian music, I hear true stories of struggles, faith, redemption, and joy. That is why I converted to this genre of music over secular music.

I was attending my first Christian music festival in Maine. I looked around me, and for once, I saw family members, not strangers. These were all children of God that I would be able to spend eternity with. Instead of being a stranger in the crowd, we were invited to meet the artists who humbled themselves and let down their pride. I met bands that I looked up to and realized that they were just like me, and God saw us both equally. Even though they were well-known and attained more income than I did, God saw us the same. I came to think that if these people standing before me could excel in their dreams and share God's heart with the world so can everyone else. As Christians, we can pray for God to help us manage our dreams if they are according to His will. (Here's me with Neal Cameron of Kutless.)

After I met the Christian recording artists, I walked outside to where the stage stood. It seemed small considering the amount of people that were there, but the stage was not even the focal point. Surrounding the stage were mountains. Beautiful mountains that seemed to touch the sky and shimmer with green pigment. There is a song by for KING & COUNTRY called "Shoulders" that immediately came into my train of thought when my eyes drifted off into the landscape.

https://itunes.apple.com/us/artist/for-king-country/id457871289

The introduction of the song is speaking and is derived from Psalm 121:1:

"I look up to the mountains. Does my strength come from the mountains? No. My strength comes from God, who made heaven and earth, and the mountains."

This introduction said exactly what was on my mind. If these mountains were so astonishing, and God has the authority to move them, just imagine how absolutely extraordinary God is. I do not think that our minds can fully grasp even the slightest concept of how amazing our creator is.

Side note: if you are a Christian music fanatic like me, check out these two festivals!

River Rock festival: http://riverrockfestival.com/
SoulFest: http://thesoulfest.com/

After that music festival, I attended a separate event in my home state of New Hampshire. There was a much larger crowd this time, yet I still felt grateful that I was spending time with others who shared my same beliefs.

My state is known for having astounding views of mountains, and this particular concert happened to be held on a mountain. That night, we had a gorgeous candlelight service and the same thoughts were going through my mind as they had before. If God is greater than all these earthly things, I cannot imagine how incredible He is. At this festival, I grew closer to my family and was humbled even more. One of my favorite memories at this venue was being in a crowd with people whom I had never met prior to this. I felt free, raising my arms up with the sense of joy in knowing that I could surrender everything to God. To add to this, my favorite band, Tenth Avenue North, serenaded the audience with their delightful, heart-spoken music

https://itunes.apple.com/us/artist/tenth-avenue-north/id15687749

After these two similar occurrences, I started to seek the word much more than I had been. Instead of meandering through the pages, I vigorously adjusted my mind and leaned into a new perspective. I had a burning motivation and wanted to learn as much as my mind could possibly contain. I came across many verses, and out of reading the same part of the Pentateuch over and over again, I was positive that God allowed me to have an understanding of what the text meant.

The final day of the event, we returned home. Home, this time, did not feel like home. I was no longer in a community of all believers other than my family. I was back to a social media-soaked world where others would ridicule my faith. I remembered a video I had watched that fit into the scenario:

https://www.youtube.com/watch?v=pwAY9P_izZ0

It basically explained this: Moses was called by God to save the slaves in Egypt. Moses replied to God, saying, "If I go to these people and say that God wants to liberate them, they are going to ask me what is this God's name?" So Moses asked God what His name was. God replied, "Moses, you tell them, the Lord sent you." This name in an English translation is spelled L-O-R-D. Even though this is how it is spelled in English, it was actually written originally in Hebrew. In the Hebrew language, the name is essentially four characters long. In English, it would be Y-H-V-H, but in Hebrew, it looks like this: יְהֹוָה. Some people pronounce it like "Yahweh," yet in many traditions, it is not even a word that is acceptable to be pronounced since it is so holy and mysterious. Some believed that the characters functioned as vowels in the Hebrew language and that they were breathing sounds. Ultimately, they came to a conclusion that the name was unpronounceable because the word was the sound of breathing. Back in Genesis, it talks about God breathing the breath of life into Adam. This breath is also referred to as the spirit, πνευμα (nooma) and ruach. This is why we believe that the spirit can dwell among us humans, the breath being the spirit. If the spirit is living in us, then God will give us life. So every time we breathe, we are declaring God's holy and righteous name! This finally brings me to my point. When my family and I returned home and someone would say something negative toward God to us, all I could hear was the sound of God's name as they breathed. When we are born, we breathe in and declare God's name, is it so that we die when we are unable to pronounce God's name, and we take our last breath and die? No matter the situation, God wants us to know His name. I think that this is an amazing thing. Instead of hearing others bash Christianity, God gave us an optimistic route that allows us to hear His name above all the chaos and commotion.

God gives us everything that we need to complete life. In addition to optimism, He gives us an instruction manual to our lives, the Bible. He gives us prosperity, a way of communication, love that never fails, and forgiveness. Whatever we need, we are able to lift it up in prayer and seek God for guidance and counseling.

No matter the venue, scenario, or time, God is always there by our side, and He can help us live a Christ-centered life if we open it up to Him. When we open our lives to Him, He does not want us to give a portion of it; He wants us all in. If we let God only control certain areas of our lives, our lives will be confusing and most likely have poor results. But if we give God full rein over our lives, we can be confident that He will deliver His promises upon us and that He will care for each and every one of us as His own.

Back to the theme of this chapter: the mountains. One of my favorite sermons comes from Jesus Himself that took place upon a mountain. I encourage you to read Matthew 5–7 as this is only a portion of the sermon that Jesus delivered:

> Blessed are the poor in spirit, for theirs is the kingdom of heaven.
> Blessed are those who mourn, for they will be comforted.
> Blessed are the meek, for they will inherit the earth.
> Blessed are those who hunger and thirst for righteousness, for they will be filled.
> Blessed are the merciful, for they will be shown mercy.
> Blessed are the pure in heart, for they will see God.
> Blessed are the peacemakers, for they will be called children of God.

Blessed are those who are persecuted because of righteousness, for theirs is the kingdom of heaven.
Blessed are you when people insult you, persecute you and falsely say all kinds of evil against you because of me.
Rejoice and be glad, because great is your reward in heaven, for in the same way they persecuted the prophets who were before you." (Matthew 5:3-11 NIV)

This sermon means that we are all broken people. Even though we are all broken, God's very capable of delivering us from evil and our trespasses. It says that God will comfort and show mercy to those who repent of their sins. This portion of the scriptures is referred to as the Beatitudes, each section acting as a proverb-like proclamation. I believe that these verses are a way that we can immensely grow in the grace of God.

Jesus depicts blessings that are precise and full of meaning right before our very eyes. If we want to grow close to God, we are able to ask Him to allow us to live out these attitudes and teach us to fulfill them to His liking. This does not mean that as Christians, we can show one example of this and then become proficient in that category. The Beatitudes are a lifestyle that God wants us to indulge in for eternity. The Beatitudes are a way that we should be carrying our Christian hearts for the rest of our lives. No matter what we hear about the Beatitudes from anyone or anything, the only way that we can truly live them out is if we ask God to mentor us in our journey of learning them.

Are you ready to climb your mountain? I have hiked many mountains in my life, the most challenging one being Mount Monadnock.

It is a 3,166 foot tall mountain that stands in Jaffrey, New Hampshire. I remember finally reaching the top of the mountain with my dad and brother, only to discover that we still needed to trek an even steeper part of the mountain to reach the top. Another time, I was camping at Mount Cardigan with a group from my former school. We went through injuries and fatigue, and we finally reached the top as a team. The year before that, I had scaled Pack Monadnock twice, and Mount Bog with my camp group. These mountain treks were all very strenuous, so why do it? The view. Once I reach the top of any mountain, I always realize that it was well worth the climb. You can see for miles on end in every direction and bathe in the glory of the beauty of the land surrounding you. So are you ready to climb your mountain? I am not talking about a physical mountain that you choose to climb for leisure. I am talking about life. There will always be obstacles in life that are mandatory to overcome in order to get by, or else we give up. We cannot necessarily choose the mountains that we climb in life, but we can choose how we climb them. Maybe you're going through an illness, a loss in your family, whatever the brokenness may be, do not give up. God has given us these trials because He knows that we can overcome them with Him.

There is a phrase that many Christians say that goes like this, "God will not give you more than you can handle." This is not valid. The truth is, God will give us way more than we can handle. The positive side is, with God, we can get through these trials. We can't do anything without God, but with Him, we can overcome things that we would never dream of overcoming. God gives us more than we can handle so that we can seek Him and He can show us that He loves us. He will provide us with the power we need to get through the obstacles instead of us trying to accomplish them on our own.

When we are tired and worn and feel like giving up, we can seek God to give us our second wind. In track, we call a second wind, a "runner's high." A runner's high is when you are about to give up, but you open your lungs up, keep breathing, and continue. You will suddenly get energy that you never knew was in you, and you can travel an even farther distance than you initially intended. So why not do the same with our faith? My pastor was preaching about this very topic today. When we are overwhelmed and ready to give up, why don't we ask God to give us a "second wind"? If we open up to Him and breathe in His spirit, we can overcome anything and continue on in life even when we lose hope and think that it might be impossible to advance any further. We can climb any mountain that is placed in our path if we open up to our creator and ask Him to fuel us with the Holy Spirit. No matter the height, distance, or incline of the obstacle, we can manage to reach the top. Below are a few examples from the book of Psalms that talk about mountains. They are beautiful verses that can have different meanings.

- "You answer us with awesome and righteous deeds, God our savior, the hope of all the ends of the earth and of the farthest seas, who formed the mountains by your power, having armed yourself with strength, who stilled the roaring seas, the roaring of their waves, and the turmoil of the nations" (Psalm 65:5–7 NIV). This verse says that God formed everything on the earth and that He has the power to do anything.

- "May the mountains bring prosperity to the people, the hills the fruit of righteousness" (Psalm 72:3 NIV). Earlier, I was explaining how our "mountain" is a trial in our life. If we replace "mountains" in this passage with "obstacles," it would say that our obstacles bring prosperity to the people and will be rewarding, which I believe is true. God knows how our lives will work out, and He makes all things work together for our good.
- "You are radiant light, more majestic than mountains rich with game" (Psalm 76:4 NIV). This is a verse purely pertaining to how amazing God is. He is filled with light and displays it for all to gaze upon.
- "I lift my eyes up to the mountains—where does my help come from?" (Psalm 121:1 NIV) I mentioned this verse earlier, and it is one of my favorites. Our help does not come from the mountains; our help and strength comes from God who created the earth and everything inside of it.
- "As the mountains surround Jerusalem, so the LORD surrounds His people both now and forevermore" (Psalm 125:2 NIV). This verse is one that should give us comfort. This analogy explains that the magnificent and mighty mountains surround Jerusalem, and God does the same to His people. No matter where we are in life, God is always there with us and will stay by our side to comfort us.

Chapter 3 Reflection

- Was there ever a place where you felt like you were home outside of your actual home?
- Is there a song that reminds you that God loves and cares for you?
- Have you ever climbed a mountain? Was the view at the end worth it?
- Are you reliant on God and His spirit to help you through your "mountains"?

JOURNALING AND PRAYERS

CHAPTER FOUR

The Longest Summer Ever

You have anticipation while staring at the clock in your class-room. It's getting closer and closer to the time that school will soon end. It is the last day of school. The homework will end, you will be allowed to sleep in, it seems amazing. Not for me. I admit, I had pretty high expectations entering the summer of 2015. I thought that I would see my friends, go to the beach, have a wonderful time at camp, and sleep in every day. Well, it did not exactly work out like that.

The first day of summer began, and I was already upset. Someone I was close to was switching schools, and all I wanted to do was hang out with them. I did sleep in, which was the highlight of my summer at this point.

Then the e-mail came. I read the headline and thought to myself, "Oh no." I clicked on it twice, and it proceeded to tell me that I had summer homework. I did not want summer homework but decided to get it done soon so that I wouldn't have to think about it. My mom purchased the book for me, and I finished reading it in about three days. (Okay, so I enjoyed the book.) I finished the attached worksheet and was excited because I had been one of the first people to finish out of my friends. Little did I know, summer homework was the least of my problems.

The rest of the week was somewhat okay. The following week, I spent the day at my aunt's house. She recently moved in the last week, but I loved her house. She lived in an old Girl Scout retreat where the houses were large cabins that had hardwood floors and A-frame architecture. We went to her pool and relaxed for the day. We decided to go to Canobie Lake Park, an amusement park in New Hampshire. At first, I didn't want to go on any thrill rides, but I caved in and ended up going on the scariest ride in the park.

As we were switching rides, my aunt received a phone call from my dad. He said that he had gone to the hospital to get some tests done and that he was currently still there. We did not think much of it, but I was a little worried at the moment. My grandparents offered for me to stay overnight at their house, but my aunt ended up staying over at my house because we got home so late. When we got back, we were informed of some frightening news.

My dad was still at the hospital, and there was something wrong. My grandparents took me to the hospital the next day. At the hospital, we heard even worse news. The MRI (magnetic resonance imaging) had revealed that my dad had experienced a stroke. The doctors could not detect the time of the stroke, so they were uncertain of how recent it had been. My grandparents were very supportive and took care of me during this length of time because my mom had been out of the state for a business trip and my brother was out of the state with his friend. I was very worried for my dad's health and I wanted him to be safe. When my mom was informed of the news, she got the next available airplane back to New Hampshire. She got home late that night and I remember hugging her and praying.

The next day, the news was even worse. Along with the stroke, my dad suffered from a VAD (vertebral artery dissection). My entire family was anxious and worried. We all wanted my dad to be safe and healthy.

During those few days, I remember searing pain in my stomach due to an intestinal disorder that I have that is brought on by anxiety.

I didn't understand why everything around me was getting worse and worse.

Finally, my brother returned home, and my mom started to inform our friends and family of what had happened.

The support that was given to my family was amazing. I think that this was an especially wonderful thing toward my parents because I was used to seeing them help everyone around them, and now they were being helped.

This time made my family grow closer and further in our faith as a family. I remember almost everyone we knew supporting our family with prayers, meals, visits, and love. Teachers, friends, coworkers, people who we hadn't even met, were helping my family in every way possible. In that moment, I saw what a Christian community is supposed to look like. On Facebook, many people said that they would pray for our family, and I believe that my dad recovered quickly because of this. Dropping what they were doing, they took the time to pray for healing upon my dad and for comfort within my family.

"And let us consider how we may spur one another on toward love and good deeds, not giving up meeting together, as some are in the habit of doing, but encouraging one another—and all the more as you see the day approaching." (Hebrews 10:24–25 NIV)

After this experience, there was a different medical emergency in our family. My cousin, only a toddler, was being airlifted to Boston Children's Hospital after multiple seizures. There was a possibility that she might not survive, but with the gathering of community once again, we all prayed, and God protected her and stayed by their family, even surrounding them with medical professionals on a crowded beach where the seizures began! Her prognosis was uncertain, but now at two years old, she's walking, gaining skills every day, and is thriving.

More and more things were coming at me and my family, but they never took us down; they only made us stronger with God in the lead.

After these two events, another one was headed toward me. My friend who was switching schools started contacting me less and less until we stopped talking altogether. I felt like I was of no value, and I was confused why this kept happening to me. Then I got my "second wind," and I accepted the fact that no matter what happens in my life, God works everything together for my good.

Ever since then, I have been stronger in my faith, and my family has been encouraging one another more and more to let God take care of us.

"Cast all your anxiety on Him because He cares for you." (1 Peter 5:7)

This verse tells us that we do not need to live in constant fear of anything. We do not need to worry about being pretentious or worry about what fate may come because we have a father who loves us so much that He sent His one and only child to die for us. He now calls us His children and has immaculate love for us. God wants us to be healthy and in good mental condition, so we do not need to worry about a single thing. I think that our society tells us to be worried if you don't conform to this definition of perfect that does not actually exist. No one has a perfect life. We are all broken people, and we need to accept the exclusive fact that God knows what He is doing.

"Fear is just a lie." (Tenth Avenue North)

I think that as humans, we feel the need to create worries or trouble in our lives. We weave a worrisome concept into the details of our days even when it really was just an illusion. An example of this can be found in social media.

Have you ever been scrolling through your feed on Facebook or Instagram and come across a picture that made you cringe? You know what I mean. That pouty face selfie that makes you shudder with fury inside? That "popular" or "pretty" girl that makes you jealous? We need to get a reality check whether we are the ones posting these selfies or if we are the ones staring face-to-face with a bunch of pixels on an app. Why do we care?

Does anyone *really* care? I can't count how many times I have seen friendships or relationships crumble because of a post. If we keep adding hardships to our lives like these, will we have any time to actually enjoy our journeys? I know that you cannot make social media disappear. The drama will follow people around you; however, we can use it for good. If every Christian were to post an uplifting Bible verse or words of encouragement, joy would take the place of drama.

A different example of placing unnecessary anxiety in our lives is found in our future. This is the concept that I have struggled the most with. As humans, we always worry about what is to come. We are scared that something will go terribly wrong or a worst-case-scenario moment will arrive. Something that I always try to keep in my mind when this scares me.

"You've never failed, and you won't start now." "Oceans," Hillsong United",

https://itunes.apple.com/us/artist/hillsong-united/id79437763

Every time that I am filled with fear, I remember that God has gotten me through some brutally harsh trials and that He will continue to do so. I also pray for Him to give me peace and a sense of comfort in knowing that He is there with me. Whenever I choose to do this, I always get through whatever I was worried about, and it almost always turns out better than I had expected it to. Here are a few examples of this:

- I had a ton of homework, and there was no possible way that I would be able to finish it. The next day I woke up sick and stayed home from school where I was able to finish all my homework. Sometimes, God fixes our problems with something that we never would think of! I wouldn't have chosen to be ill, but God used it in my life for good.

- My former school was not a place that I wanted to attend anymore, but I was petrified of switching schools again. After switching, I fell in love with my new school and met people who I could actually call my friends.
- While I lived in Florida at a younger age, I was constantly bullied. My mind was not assimilating to this very well, so my teachers and family decided that it would be a good decision for me to go a grade level lower. This way, I would not see my bullies, and I would be back in a classroom with others my own age. I was not extremely keen on this idea, but I knew that it was best for me. When my family moved back to New Hampshire, I knew that that decision was made to line up perfectly for what God intended for my life. Because of that small choice, I was able to attend a mission trip where I continued on in my journey of being born again. If I had been in an upper grade level, I would not have met my best friends, I would not have been able to attend that mission trip, and my relationship with God would be nowhere near where it is today.

Even though we create fear in our lives, we can choose to create joy in our lives. If we look for the good in our lives and stop focusing on the detrimental periods of our existence, our lives will be much more sublime and gratifying. There are so many vivid pictures of God's admiration for us, we just need to take the time to go out and look for those. If all we do is mope about how terrible our lives are and we throw pity parties for ourselves, we are choosing to have a subpar life that is not sturdy or stable. If we build our lives on what God wants for us and we are thankful for what we do have, we will notice the actually incredible lives that we do have. I cannot stress this enough because I used to have a negative attitude like this. All I wanted was my life. I didn't want my life to follow any other plan than my own. But then I understood that God made my life exactly the way it is because His reasoning is so much greater than mine will ever be.

If you think that you have nothing, you are wrong. You have God no matter what your possessions may be. This was a major problem that my brother and I noticed with our previous school. There was an enormous need for people to flaunt their materialistic items around like they were all that mattered. I am not making this up; some of the students in the district made a group called the Three Car Garage Club, really? Why? All they had was money. I remember stepping off the school bus when someone told me that my house was tiny and that I was poor. This made me so upset because I knew that I was nowhere near poor. The poor people were the families that started the Three Car Garage Club, and the students who called my family poor. The poor are those who do not have God. Rich are those who seek God's love and share it with others. While visiting the Dominican Republic, I witnessed families who had no food, no shoes, and small shacks not large enough for their entire families to reside in. Even in their circumstance, they were rich. Not because of their almost nonexistent shelters or their lack of food but because of their faith. They loved God so much, and that was all that they needed. Life may be full of expensive "fancy cars," but in heaven where it counts, material items are absolutely nothing. All those people in my former school had nothing. They did not have faith. They treated others cruelly for having nothing when in reality, they were the ones with nothing.

"Sell your possessions and give to the poor. Provide purses for yourselves that will not wear out, a treasure in heaven that will never fail, where no thief comes near and no moth destroys. For where your treasure is, there your heart will be also." (Luke 12:33–34 NIV)

If you have not noticed by now, I tend to drift off into completely different topics in my manuscript. Back to the summer of 2015! Over the summer, I was going through many mundane days. I was sick of it, so I decided to finish a computer-coding course that I took up awhile ago. I didn't think that I would be able to finish, but I finished the course with plenty of time left. I didn't need to do the course, but something kept me pushing through to code for thirteen hours. I had the same experience while I was running over the summer. I did not need to run at all, but something kept me running every mile. I realized that even though I did not need to do these things, it would help me in the future. I think that we can be like this in our faith as well. If we go the extra mile to help others, God will reward us with joy in knowing that we helped someone. But if we do these things, we need to do them with love. If all our mind is focused on helping someone but our heart is not in it at all, it means nothing. In a different song, the band for KING & COUNTRY says this:

"If I speak with human eloquence and angelic ecstasy, but don't love, I'm nothing but the creaking of a rusty gate. If I speak God's word with power revealing all His mysteries and making everything as plain as day, and if I have faith to say to a mountain; "Jump!" and it jumps, but I don't love, I'm nothing. If I give all I own to the poor or even go to the stake to be burned as a martyr, but I don't love, I've gotten nowhere. So no matter what I say, no matter what I believe, no matter what I do, I'm bankrupt without love." ("The Proof of Your Love")

What I am trying to convey here is this, we should not do things with the motivation being only that we need to do them. We should do everything out of love. God talks about it this way; anything you say or do to anyone, you are doing to God. So if you choose to do something to help someone, out of love, you have made God pleased with you because you have done what He asked. If you do something so that you can get something out of it or if you do it for any self-fulfilling purpose, you are not fulfilling what God asks of you. It is as simple as this:

"Do everything in love." (1 Corinthians 16:14 NIV)

Chapter 4 Reflection

- Was there ever a time where your family needed support?
- What were some trials you have had that made you stronger in your faith?
- Why do we not need to worry?
- Why should we do things out of love and not for our own good?

JOURNALING AND PRAYERS

CHAPTER FIVE

Equal

In the beginning of eighth grade, my teacher read us a book called *The Acorn People* by Ron Jones. In the book, there were children of all ages that struggled with disabilities. They all attended a summer camp that was made for children with disabilities. The book was written from the counselor's point of view. In the beginning, the counselor was not very keen on the concept, but in the end, he appreciated how amazing it actually was. The kids who felt like they did not belong helped each other throughout the week and even managed to climb a mountain together.

For most of my class, I do not think that the book made an especially large impact on them, but to me it did. My mom had worked as a para ever since I was born, and I had seen children with special needs treated cruelly at school by students. I remember noticing a student walking down the hall that my mom had worked with. She was very polite and said hello to two girls standing by their lockers. Instead of being kind, they did not respond and continued talking. After seeing this, I was really upset. Just because these girls fit into the society's "norm" does not mean that they can bully others.

The girl had special needs, but that did not make her a different person. God sees us the same in His eyes, and I did not understand the cruelty behind those girls.

After witnessing this event, I went over to the girl and had a very nice conversation with her. I had acknowledged that my mom knew her, and she seemed very grateful that I had talked to her. She should not need to be grateful for something like that, but because of our society treating her differently, she does not expect to be treated like a human being. I think that is terrible and pathetic.

I kept noticing similar occurrences in my school, and it was making me very upset. Eventually, I switched schools, and the occurrences ended. It did not change the fact that it was still happening, and I needed clarification that somewhere on the earth, teens were treating others who had disabilities with equality. I waited for a while, and then the day came.

My mom had switched jobs in the beginning of the year. She now works for a ministry organization called Joni and Friends that encourages the faith of anyone with disabilities.

http://www.joniandfriends.org/new-england/

I was not exactly sure what she did at work until I was able to experience it firsthand. The company is very large, and workers can range from California, all the way to New England. The company was started after a woman named Joni Eareckson Tada began her journey. She had been in an accident that paralyzed her body from the neck down. (There is a movie called *Joni* that I highly recommend.) Joni was very discouraged but then started living in her faith and getting stronger each day. She is an incredible woman who now runs Joni and Friends and helps many people internationally who have disabilities.

The first day that I volunteered at Joni and Friends, I had no idea what to expect. I walked in the office and began a mailing project that I was told to work on. The item that was being mailed was an invitation to a dinner that Joni would be attending and speaking at. On every invitation, there was a picture of a girl with an STM (short-term missionary). I later found out that the picture was taken at a retreat for those with disabilities. The girl who was in a wheel-chair was with an STM who serves as a friend who acts like a one-on-one counselor/mentor. Once I heard of the retreat, I was intrigued. I thought that is was amazing that these people and their families could visit a place all together where they felt like they belonged.

The next day that I volunteered, my mom took me up to the retreat on the day that the campers arrived. We welcomed the camp-ers and were able to experience a golf cart tour of the camp with a really cool guy. The STMs were all around my age or in their teens. I knew that they had a heart for God because while talking to some of them, they all mentioned that they are blessed to be a part of some-thing like that. There were campers running around, talking to one another, and just being kids! When I was there, I was so grateful to be a part of experiencing this wonderful sanctuary where no one felt set apart or different. Then I remembered that heaven will be that way. Everyone will be so focused on worshipping God that no one will be excluded and everyone will be welcomed into the kingdom.

The next day, I volunteered in the office with my mom again. We talked about how amazing the camp was and that we couldn't wait to go back the following day. I woke up in the morning excited to see what the camp would offer that day. I worked in the office for a while with my mom, and then we ventured off into the wooded areas of New Hampshire until we came across the serene camp again. We drove in and parked the car. There was a talent show scheduled at seven, which was one reason why we wanted to come that day. We entered the gymnasium and peered into a room filled with empty chairs waiting to be filled. A film crew was also setting up to film for a documentary that they were filming about a little girl who attended the retreat.

We waited for a little while until the campers started arriving. The emcee was prepared, and all the performers were as well. The acts were short yet full of meaning. The applause after each act was aston-ishing, and the joy that the audience received after seeing a bright smile on the campers' face for even a second was just remarkable. I found myself grinning the entire time and awaiting the following acts. This was the clarification that I needed. This was the place where Christians could come together and forget about their worries and focus on God. That night was a humbling, life-changing experience for me. I think that everyone at my age or even older should experience something like that. It teaches us to be inclusive and to look at someone's heart, not the outward appearance. Everyone at that camp was the same as you and me. We are all in need of God, and our God sees us all the same, equal.

"But when you give a banquet, invite the poor, the crippled, the lame, the blind, and you will be blessed. Although they cannot repay you, you will be repaid at the resurrection of the righteous." (Luke 14:13–14 NIV)

I know that this chapter is short, and the next one will be even shorter, but spend some time reflecting on that verse and answering the following questions.

Chapter 5 Reflection

- Was there ever a time when you were not inclusive?
- Do you regret that moment?
- Does God see us differently from people with disabilities?
- God sees us all equal, do you agree? Why?

JOURNALING AND PRAYERS

CHAPTER SIX

Where Are You?

Have you ever struggled with the tangible aspect of God? I know that I have, and it is one of my most faced struggles. These are some ways that help me process that God is indeed with me at all times.

- Look at this image. It is very simple; it is a circle. I don't like depicting God as the pictures we all see in coloring books or movies because God is depicted differently in different countries. If I am struggling with this, I try to think of God like this: the circle has no beginning and no end. It is always there and is whole. Then I apply this to God. God is the alpha and the omega. He is always there and is whole. I am not saying that God is a circle. I use the tangible aspects of a circle and apply them to God.

- Pray out loud. This is one thing that really helps me to visualize God's presence. If I speak out loud, I get the feeling of talking to someone and having a bonding conversation. If this doesn't work, you can even set a chair in front of you and visualize God in front of you while you're speaking. You can also get on your knees and pray. When I do this, I picture the cross standing tall above me while I am at the foot of it.

- I am guilty of this, and I am sure a lot of people are. We need to read the Bible more. The Bible is the most tangible thing on this earth that we have that leads us straight to God. He is the author of the book, and we can check what He has to say no matter what time or day it is. I always feel closer to God when I get into the word, and I know that you will too.

- Worship time. This is my all-time favorite form of feeling God's presence. Whether I sing, play guitar, keyboard, bass, or a combination of them, I always feel God's presence. Worship is a way that I can express everything on my mind in something as simple as a song. If music is not really your thing, there is also dance. Dancing is a different way you can worship God. At my school, there is a worship program that teaches students to apply their technique to glorify God.

- Running. This is my least favorite way of feeling God's presence, but I swear by it. When I run and feel like giving up, I always feel God wanting me to persevere. As I am running, my mind usually clears up, and I start thinking of verses, and I am filled with more energy.

Those are the tips that I have, but there are many more. Feeling God's presence can be found in almost anything; you just need to search long and hard for them. You can pray for God to give you peace and confidence in Him being there, and He always will be. The following chart can be a record of which tips worked for you and which did not. Write *Yes* or *No* below each category. Feel free to write down other things that were not mentioned.

Tangibility Chart / Notes and Ideas

Visualizing	Praying Out Loud	Reading the Word	Worship	Running/Exercising

Other ideas:

Notes:

JOURNALING AND PRAYERS

CHAPTER SEVEN

Strike

As I currently type my heart away, there is a thunderstorm taking place. There is darkness for a few seconds, and then light comes in from what seems like every direction. For a split second, everything is visible to the eye. Followed by the light, there is a tremendous roar coming forth from the sky. The rain pelts down on the blacktop and ripples across windows in our house. The thunder is never expected; it can happen at any given moment in time. You can feel the entire house vibrate as a bolt enters the atmosphere. It seems like a typical movie scene except it is realistic. The reality it brings is extraordinary. It reminds us that we are not in control and that something much greater is before us.

No one knows the day or the hour of which Jesus will return. It is said that He will come like lightning and strike at any moment. My heart thuds another time as a bolt is heard loud among my neighborhood. I have a reality check that tells me that Jesus is coming. He could come as I am typing this, tomorrow, next week, any time.

"But about the day or hour no one knows, not even the angels in heaven, nor the son, but only the Father." (Matthew 24:36 NIV)

"'Look, He is coming with the clouds,' and 'every eye will see Him, even those who pierced Him'; and all peoples on the earth 'will mourn because of Him.' So shall it be! Amen." (Revelation 1:7 NIV)

"For the Lord Himself will come down from heaven, with a loud command, with the voice of the archangel and with the trumpet call of God, and the dead in Christ will rise first. After that, we who are still alive and left will be caught up together with them in the clouds to meet the Lord in the air. And so we will be with the Lord forever." (1 Thessalonians 4:16–17 NIV)

"And if I go and prepare a place for you, I will come back and take you to be with me that you may also be where I am." (John 14:3 NIV)

"'I am the Alpha and the Omega,' says the Lord God, 'who is, and who was, and who is to come, the almighty.'" (Revelation 1:8 NIV)

These verses clearly tell us that our Lord is coming back for us. The only one who knows when is our Father. It could happen in our generation, or millions of generations later, and we need to be prepared. If Jesus came right this moment, would you be ready? As Christians, we need to reach as many people as we possibly can in the shortest period of time. We need to stop procrastinating and work on furthering the kingdom of God immediately. Think, if Jesus came and you were saved but you put in no effort to help your friends get saved, would they spend eternity with you and God?

We are in a spiritual battle every single day. If we even get caught off guard for a second, we could damage our faith. We should cry out to God and stand firm in our faith because we have no idea when Jesus is coming back.

Do not be someone who stays behind. Know your God and share Him with everyone around you. Reflect Jesus through the way you live and do not fall into temptation. God knows that we will struggle and sometimes fail, but that certainly does not and will never change His love for us. If we seek Him first and fix our eyes on the truth, God will surely provide a way for us to escape temptation and sin.

I am so grateful that I have been given a way out of my sin. I still sin constantly, but while seeking God's word and His wisdom, I am learning to repent of my sins. It is so important that we share God with everyone before it is too late. We were not meant to wander the earth and stay quiet to ourselves. We were made to shine, be courageous, and live for so much more than we do. If we do not spread God's love, there will be less and less Christians, and eventually the world will be filled with doubt. It is already turning to a doubtful society, so we need to do something about it as fast as we possibly can. It does not matter if you are young, old, rich, poor, weak, or strong. We were all meant to complete the same mission, which is to put the love that we have received into everyone around us so that they may know the God that we came to know.

When Jesus comes and asks you why you deserve to go to heaven, what would be your response? (Think about it; this will be reestablished in the chapter reflection.) I have spent a great deal of time considering this, and this is what my response would look like.

"Jesus, I do not deserve this at all. In fact, I deserve the worst. Until you came, there was no hope for me. I would have been sent to hell where I would burn for eternity. But you provided a way out. You bridged the gap of sin with the cross on which you had to bear my sins. I am immensely grateful for the new person that you have made me to be, and I cannot express that enough. Instead of counting my good deeds versus my transgressions, you look at the inward appearance, my heart. You have removed my transgressions from as far as the east is from the west so that I may get the privilege of being with you for eternity. That is why heaven is in reach for me. You have given me the privilege of becoming your daughter and living with you in your kingdom forever."

"Therefore, there is now no condemnation for those who are in Christ Jesus." (Romans 8:1)

We can enter heaven by grace alone. Our pride will only bring us down and will get us nowhere in life. If we are active in our relationship with God, we can be confident that there is hope and salvation for our lives. No matter how badly you have messed up or how deep a hole that you have dug yourself into, there is always a way out. God has already forgotten about your sins, so there is no need to hold on to them. God will forgive you if you ask Him, and He will offer new life and a realm of possibility. One of the misconceptions about heaven is that you get in by doing good things. This contradicts the Bible entirely because God tells us that our deeds make no impact on whether or not we will gain entry in heaven. The only way to reach heaven is through Jesus, who made a way for us on the cross. He sacrificed His pure, unblemished life for us so that we could live free and love strong like He did. God's not mad at you, nor will He ever be. He sent His son to die for you because of how much He loves you. Your life is valuable to God, and He will never leave you nor forsake you.

Do not procrastinate in your faith. Many have said that they want to "get right with God" before they go to Him, but God says no! He wants you to come as you are and repent as soon as possible. If you try to repent before going to God, you will be a mess. God wants us to seek Him for forgiveness so that He may help us as we repent of our sins.

Some even make excuses that Christianity did not work for them or that church is just too much of a commitment. But I say this; God never said, "Thou must go to church every Sunday." But shouldn't you want to go to church? It's the least that we could do since God gave up His son for us.

Christianity is the only way, so when people say that it didn't work out, are they implying that the route of not believing was working out better for them?

There are many stereotypes given to Christians for being Goodie Two-shoes, but I think that is bologna. Christians are all sinners; we just chose to ask God to forgive us. Many atheists take pride in accusing us when we slip up because they believe that we are prideful in our good deeds. If anything, I think that atheists are prideful in their deeds and we are to be humble toward them.

Along with the stereotypes, there are often questions that Christians can be asked. Here are a few examples:

I was sitting in my classroom reading my bible when a boy walked up to me. I was confused because we had never talked before. Then he said this, "Why are you reading a dictionary?" Really? A dictionary? I told him that it was a bible, and he simply walked away.

After a girl in front of me heard that I was reading a bible, she quickly turned around and asked this, "Are you religious or something?" I told her that I was a Christian, and she had a strange look on her face. (Side note: My Christian faith is not a religion. It's a relationship I have with God.) She proceeded to ask me why I was reading the bible, and I told her that I wanted to because it was a main part of my faith. She seemed shocked and said, "I thought that your parents forced you to read it or something."

These are just a few things associated with being a Christian. Some people think that Christians are all prissy people who are "perfect" at abiding by the rules. They think that everyone else is being bombarded for their unbelief when the reality is, Christians take a lot of brutality for believing in God, and it can be hard sometimes. This is another reason why we need to stand our ground. This world tries to get us away from God in every way it can so that we will not be able to add our peers into the kingdom. Temptation leads us out of our faith and into this dark world that we live in. If you look around you, what do you see? Secular music trashing women, protests all over the country, social media pills, and inappropriate advertisement. Our world is becoming more corrupt by the second. More and more people are starting to conform to the patterns of this world, and it is getting more dangerous as time goes by. It is a crucial time for Christians right now because we may be the only way anyone finds out about God. With distractions everywhere, we can find ourselves consumed by tabloids and false accusations. If we surround ourselves with the gospel and encouraging people, it will be easier to stand our ground. This can be hard to do in this generation, but God is always there and is in control.

No matter what people say to you, know that God is watching and that you are on His side. Our biggest fear is being different, so people will try to discriminate against you in any way possible, so we need to fight back with love.

"But I tell you, love your enemies and pray for those who persecute you." (Matthew 5:44 NIV)

It may seem unconventional at first, but if we share love with others, they will start to see Jesus reflecting off us, and they may long to know Him.

The storm has ended, and there is a sense of peace over the city. As I type, I am drowsy and look forward to rest. God can give this to us. When He comes back, He will take the steadfast in their faith with Him and will give them rest. There will be peace at last, and we will be able to rest in His arms.

Chapter 7 Reflection

- Are you ready for Jesus to come back?
- How should you handle being persecuted for your faith?
- Why are Christian stereotypes unrealistic?
- If Jesus asked you why you deserved to go to heaven, what would you say to Him?

Journaling and Prayers

CHAPTER EIGHT

Adventure

My high school recently attended a retreat where we bonded with each other as a body of Christ. I was not sure what to expect, so I kept a clear mind-set. I knew that there would be some obstacles on the trip, but I also knew that God would help me get through them all. I had just stayed up until two in the morning while trying to finish a computer science course, and I could not fall asleep after that. That night, I remember struggling a bit to feel God's presence. For some reason, I couldn't fall asleep at all. The following day, our high school stayed overnight at our school so that we could leave early in the morning to go to the retreat. We had a nice time and played some dodgeball and other assorted games while in fellowship. Before bed, I remember thinking that I could not wait to get a good night's rest. I finally fell asleep, and then I was awoken by severe stomach pain. I thought to myself that this was going to be the worst trip of my life, and my optimism shut off like a switch. I barely got any rest, and I was nearing the stages of sleep deprivation. I fell asleep once again and had a grand total of three hours of sleep. At 4:30 AM, the lights were turned on, and my stomach was still killing me. I packed up my belongings and proceeded to the bus. My friend and I reached one of the two buses, and we were informed that there was not enough room on that bus, so we needed to go on the other one. We went to the other bus, and they said that only one of us could fit. Guess who was the last high schooler in the group? Me. I waddled over to my church's bus that my school was borrowing, and I climbed on. The entire ride, my stomach would not settle, and I was on the verge of yelling at my brother to be quiet.

But I kept my cool. We passed toll booth after toll booth until we finally reached Maine. A girl who I wanted to get to know sat in my seat, and we learned that we had a lot in common with each other. I remember the two of us peering out of the small window, gazing upon the serenity of the mountains. I even forgot about the pain!

Sometimes we like to blame our pain and sorrows on God, but we need to remember that God had a perfect plan for each and every one of our lives. God gave us free will, which unfortunately brought sin in our lives, and many have a misconception that God caused our suffering. God despises our suffering and provides a way out for us in everything. I am not sure, but I think that maybe pain can help us appreciate the amazing lives that we already live. Our lives will be difficult at moments, but God's timing is absolutely spotless, and we were never destined to suffer.

Once we reached the camp, all the students on my bus glimpsed out of our opened windows and gazed at the layout of the outpost. On the way, the upperclassmen and the lowerclassmen talked about not separating into different cabins, and some were not keen on the thought, but in the end, I think that it played an important role in our trip.

We drove down the gravel path to a massive structure made out of beautiful wood material. When we entered the cabin, it smelled like cedar and was in mint condition. I plopped my several belongings on a mattress and proceeded outside to see what was going on. I met up with my friends, and we walked down the rocky path to what seemed to be the dining hall.

The aroma of lunch was fresh in our nostrils, but my stomach and my taste buds did not agree with each other. I was in agony all day, and I just wanted to relax.

Sometimes we need a break and feel like we cannot handle something. It happens to everyone at some point, but remember this, God has catered every single thing to fit your life wholly, so even the days of doubt and frustration serve a purpose. That is why we cannot set a plan for ourselves. If we have an idea of what we want for our future but don't let God step in, we aren't living for God's will; we're living for us. A song that I have grown fond toward demonstrates how we should be living. It's very simple:

"More of you, less of me, make me who I'm meant to be. You're all I want, all I need, you're everything. Take it all, I surrender, be my king."

"More of You" by Colton Dixon,
https://itunes.apple.com/us/artist/colton-dixon/id508624868

So we gave thanks and ended our meal. Following lunch, there was an academic challenge that was set up by our headmaster. We were told to create a container that could hold a rock. It had to somehow be thrown into the water over a long distance and manage to float, but not float too much. As my group discussed our plan, we looked at the other groups, and it seemed that they all had a similar approach. We were the outsiders with the large box that might be impossible to get into the water. We constructed our "container," and it was our team's turn to test our product. We could not think of a way to get our box into the water other than throwing it, so I was supposed to summon all my strength and catapult our rock container into the water. We had almost no hope. I threw it, and it hit the dock. But then since our container did not allow the rock to settle in a specific place, it shifted and rolled barely into the water.

This may seem odd, but have you ever felt like the rock, being thrown over a distance that you're not sure you will make? I certainly have, and it can be menacing when you face an obstacle as such. But unlike my group's lack of hope in our structure, we can have confidence in our God. God can shift our lives and let them fall into place. When we think that everything is coming apart, what if it is actually coming together?

It was now free time. I met up with the girl whom I chatted with, and we formed a small worship session. I was now in a group with three other girls whom I had not had a chance to spend time with at school. Even though it was small, I think that it was one of the biggest blessings on our trip. We spent our time praising the Lord as a community of believers and raising our hands to God.

We can get so caught up in distractions in our life, that we don't remember the little things that blessed us. If we keep focusing on all the negativity that was brought up in our day, we can lose all the amazing memories of love, joy, peace, patience, kindness, goodness, gentleness, and faithfulness that was woven into our day in many different places.

Free time came to a close, and it was now time for the main worship session by the campfire. Staring at the fire, I could hear each individual spark burst after hitting oxygen. The foggy smoke bellowed up to the sky, and the light flickered and turned our cheeks rosy and warm. Our voices intertwined in harmonies and melodies, some singing lower and higher octaves. Even though we all had a different voice, we were all singing in unity, and every lyric was intended to praise the same loving God that created us.

We all have different voices, different opinions, and different backgrounds. Even though this is true, as believers, we are the body of Christ. We have a say in decisions here on earth. We choose who enters the kingdom of heaven, and we can either refuse entry or be welcoming and loving like we were made to be.

That night, I slept astonishingly. I woke up eager to spend more time in community. Now was the main event of our trip, white-water rafting. I consider myself pretty adventurous, so I was very excited. It took awhile to reach the river, but eventually we made it and geared up. We trekked our giant yellow flotation device down to a dam and placed it ever so gently into the flowing river. Once we climbed aboard, we were given commands that were expected to be fulfilled. At some times, it was hard to keep in sync with one another, but we were all receiving the same commands.

Sometimes, our approaches may vary, but we can listen to God who gives us the true commands. If you fix your eyes on Him, He can and will provide you with the knowledge and strength that you need to perform tasks.

I almost fell into water, but I didn't. At one point, our guide told us that we were allowed to swim in the rapids. As the adventurous person I am, I decided that I was going to participate, and I even convinced a couple others on my raft to join me in the duration of our trip. It turned out to be one of the most incredible things that I have ever done. After that, we stopped for lunch and finally returned back to camp. (This is me and my friends white-water rafting).

Here is the link to where my high school stayed in Maine: mooseriveroutpost.com

Here is the link to the rafting company: adv-bound.com/content/dead-river-maine-whitewater-rafting for the rafting

That night, we had yet another amazing encounter with God. Our leader had generously organized different and well-thought-out stations that gave an activity. We split up into groups of three to five and started on a selected station. I started at an activity in which my group made words that described God. After we did this, looking at the words gave a visual and tangible way to experience what God is. Some of our words included *Alpha, Omega, forever, daddy, love,* and *redeemer.* This exercise helped me as a visual learner to understand how God can be described, and I recommend jotting down some words of your own to try it for yourself.

At the next station, we molded an idol that we had a hard time demolishing. When we finished, we destroyed the clay that we used to make our "idols." The next activity was about posture that we could use in prayer. I know that some felt strange doing these certain things, but I believe that it had an impact on my worship. We first raised our hands above our heads and prayed. We repeated prayer as we kneeled, got down on our faces, and then ended.

The next station had the biggest impact on our particular group. We each took a piece of string and cut it in half with shears to symbol a broken relationship that we had in the past. We then tied the two halves of the strings together and placed them on the cross followed by prayer. There were tears that led to powerful discussions, and I felt blessed to be a part of it. The service ended, and our group went and sat under the stars. Again, I felt so small and recognized that God put detail into every single one of the millions of stars, so He must care about me more than I ever knew He could.

I slept great again that night, and the next morning, we boarded the buses once again. It was a little bittersweet dismissing our trip, but the time that we spent there was a blessing. On our returning trip, we blared my favorite Christian radio station through the bus, and we sang to our lungs' capacity. A melancholy part of our return drive would have to be seeing a deceased moose lying in the center of the road. (Other than that, our return trip went well.)

When we returned to school, we sanitized the bus and took out the Dunkin' Donuts-filled trash can. (There is literally a Dunkin' Donuts every five miles in New England.) The middle schoolers had left bright, pastel, sticky notes on our lockers with lovely notes written atop them. It was nice to experience community even when we returned back at school.

The next week was hectic. I started singing on the worship team. I started having cross-country practice, and the homework pile came rolling in.

My stress skyrocketed through the ceiling, and eventually I needed a break. I had not made enough time for God, and everything seemed like a mess. One night, I went home and prayed to God about everything that was on my mind. It was amazing to feel all my stress release by simply confessing everything to God.

"Do not be anxious about everything, but in every situation, by prayer and petition, with thanksgiving, present your requests to God." (Philippians 4:6 NIV)

Chapter 8 Reflection

- Do you ever feel like you need a break?
- How can we improve our day?
- If we notice the little blessings, will our lives be more positive?
- When was a time that you felt closer to God and a sense of community?

Journaling and Prayers

CHAPTER NINE

Testimony

Every year, our school assigns a long-term project that we are allowed to choose. For one particular year, my brother and I chose to create a video in which we recorded our family's testimonies. Here's the link to the video we made.

https://www.youtube.com/watch?v=cg6j-c3z4Ag

Since then, my personal testimony has been added, and there were several testimonies in the video that I wanted to share; hence this chapter is solely dedicated to those testimonies. To start out, here is my testimony so that there will be more insight as you read this manuscript:

> Dear Diary, today was petrifying, and I don't think that I can do this anymore. I am perplexed as to why they are treating me like this, and I cannot comprehend why I am even presently here right now. My wrists have shallow gashes that I don't feel like reopening, but I'm also too weak to get down on my callous knees. Moving states

has not done much for my situation. My best friend's sister just died at fifteen, and my other best friend is trying to take her own life. Why is death so near to a youthful generation?

Temptation is calling me and I want to refuse, but sometimes it sinks in just a little too deep for me to ignore it. I feel like I can't talk to my family because they are all dealing with their own sorrows, so what do I do?

"There is a time for everything, and a season for every activity under the heavens" (Ecclesiastes 3:1 NIV)

God's formulation is absolutely perfect. When we think that something has gone haywire in our lives, God can morph our situation into something cordial in the future. We just need to persist in our patience and let God execute His will. When I was struggling through some of the trials in my life, God used them later down the line and shaped me into the divergent being that I am today. At the time, I did not acknowledge that things would improve, but in God's timing, the things that were negative to me were molding my future into something much more prominent.

I used to go through the motions of Christianity every day while managing to not grasp a single aspect of what I was doing. Growing up, I did not know that God had a purpose for my life. I used to be the most effervescent, outgoing little girl with a childlike faith that could move mountains. All of that seemed to vanish once I reached the double digits, and things took an immense turn for the worse. At that time, I was so focused on the vigorous trials that would encompass my mundane life that I lost God as my limelight and focal point. The excerpt above demonstrates only a glimpse into the dark world in which I used to reside.

I reached such a level of depressed and deranged thoughts that I considered ending my life and harming myself, but something kept me from executing those terrible things time and time again. I knew that I could never go through with it because it would be narcissistic, and a part of me wanted to persevere and demolish the antagonist that I had become. Little did I know, when I thought that my world was falling apart, it was settling in place. As strange as it sounds, I think this verse resembles how I was feeling at this moment in time:

"When the sun rose, God provided a scorching east wind, and the sun blazed on Jonah's head so that he grew faint. He wanted to die, and said, 'It would be better for me to die than to live.'" (Jonah 4:8 NIV)

Maybe I was not as blatant as Jonah, but I definitely did not feel like pursuing my current situation.

His timing is unmarred. In that void period of my life, I was tormented by others in my grade constantly. I always felt like the minority, and as soon as I would get home, I would slam my door and cry out warm tears as I sobbed. Eventually it reached a point where I joined the grade level lower for the sole purpose that I wouldn't be bullied anymore. I knew that my life would change drastically, but I didn't know how or when. From that one decision to change a grade level, I was able to have many experiences that I would not have had if I were to remain in the same grade level.

I moved back to New Hampshire from Florida in 2011. My parents compelled me to join a youth group, which altered my life. There was a retreat that we went to at Monadnock Bible Conference. There was a scheduled sermon that impacted me a great deal and ultimately led me to Christ and God's omnipresence. It was the first time that I felt a personal connection with my creator, and I longed to experience more of it.

My faith began to expand to a capacity that it never had before, but the school district that I was in did not allow me to pursue my faith. As I started to change, I also noticed things that I had never taken the time to observe. My classmates would focus on material-istic items rather than relationships, and that was all that they had. One day, I was tired of it, and I boldly asked my mother if I could change schools. My brother was not too keen on the idea, but my parents and I thought that it would benefit us greatly. That is when we started school at Mount Zion.

I will never forget the day that I began attending. I felt welcomed and not ashamed of my beliefs, economic situation, looks, or anything. Soon, nothing mattered except for God. I felt like God was telling me that I could relax and live the life that I was meant to. Going to Mount Zion has been the biggest blessing in my life. I am so fortunate to attend the school, and I am glad that I made the decision to transfer.

Within a month or so at school, I was asked if I could go on a mission trip to the Dominican Republic. While I was there, I received an e-mail that confirmed my faith in Jesus Christ. The e-mail was from Mrs. Seward, and it said that she had a dream about me and that I could sing. I had been praying to God to give me an opportunity to sing because it was my favorite form of worship, and He had sent me the passion to praise Him through song. The e-mail hit me so emotionally, and my eyes were opened to the steadfast amazement that God had heard my prayers. I also realized that God had brought me to that exact place at that exact time. When I got bullied while I was younger and I moved down a grade, it had allowed me to be on that mission trip at that precise date.

After that e-mail, I fully accepted the eternal life that Jesus had given to me on the cross. I developed a spark of faith that I never knew existed in me. I did things that I would have never done such as singing at eighth-grade graduation, joining the high school worship team, teaching myself how to play guitar and pair it with songs of gratitude, engaging in the word, and talking to God on a regular basis. I am not the same person, and I am enjoying the new me a whole lot better than my preterite self.

"Jesus replied, 'Very truly I tell you, no one can see the kingdom of God unless they are born again.'" (John 3:3 NIV)

I have been born again as a daughter of the King, and I know that God was and is working through everything in my life for a greater purpose pertaining to my future. I have started my journey on the path that God wants me to take. I believe in God with every part of my flesh and soul that is filled with the breath of life. I long for more of God and less of me. Currently, I do not know what my specific purpose in life is, but with every opportunity that I receive, I will give my all so that I may extend the kingdom of God to others. I am moving out of my life and dying to self. I want to let God take over my future and renew my life.

"But those who wait on the Lord shall renew their strength; They shall mount up with wings like eagles, They shall run and not be weary, They shall walk and not faint." (Isaiah 40:31 NKJV)

So with every step that I take and every breath that enters my system, I know that God has intended it and that He is fabricating something ravishing to look upon that is imminent for my relationship between Him and me.

My testimony continues to change every day, and God adds and subtracts things from my story every day.

This next testimony was included in the video that was created last year, but I think that it is an amazing testimony, and I would like to share it.

My grandpa is a persevering man who enjoys creating beautiful wood carvings in his free time. He is a man of faith and even considered becoming a pastor at one point in his life. God has always been in his life for as long as he could remember, but there was one specific time where he felt God's presence the most. On June 5, 1991, he had just gotten his pilot's license and taken off from a small airfield in New Hampshire. He was up about eight hundred feet in the air, and the engine died completely. It had thrown a piston rod and was totally useless at that point. There was a book that came with the plane that said if you were anywhere below nine hundred feet, you are supposed to continue on straight and do the best that you can to land in an emergency situation. He was over a city and knew that there was no place to land. Against the advice of the book, he turned around. Miraculously, there was a strong wind that he was taken into, which helped carry him closer to the airport. He was gliding, staring down at the airport, which was divided by a three-foot chain-link fence. He knew that there was no possible way that he would not hit the fence. At the very last minute, he pushed down on the yoke that would allow the aircraft to pick up a little speed. He then sharply pulled back and literally bounced the wheels off the top of the fence and landed in a grassy area just before the runway.

"If God had not been there, I would have flipped over and been instantly killed. At that very moment, I promised God that I would never ever fly in a small plane again because you can do everything right and still die." (Bruce Edwards)

I would like to focus on the last point that my grandpa made. In life, we tend to subconsciously think that one day, we will not exist on this earth. When faced with reality, everything becomes more vivid and factual. In our most terrifying places, that is where we can feel God the most, so do not be discouraged. Everything in our lives is intended and serving a greater purpose to reveal God to us.

This last testimony that I am going to share with you is my mom's. She is an amazing woman, and I think that she is the best example of what a Christian mother should look like. My mom grew up as a Christian just like myself. She has always been a strong Christian, but one time in particular shaped her into who she is today. At a young age, my mom was water-skiing. She had injured her back, and although it did not alter her life as much then, it came back as she got older. One summer, her back was in the worst pain that she had ever experienced. I remember her lying on the couch, motionless and in agony.

I wanted to help her, but I didn't know what to do. That time in our lives, we prayed and prayed and prayed. It seemed like nothing was happening, but then God showed up. My mom had not been excited about the idea of surgery, but eventually, it was time for her to regain her life. She went in surgery and came out a new person. She could walk with ease after the surgery, and she was recovering very quickly. The entire thing had been a blessing and brought our family closer. I am not saying that we do not still go through tough things, but when we do, God is always there for us, and He is our provider.

God is the author of our hope, and we can let Him write our stories.

Chapter 9 Reflection

- Why is it good to examine different testimonies?
- Are you letting God write your testimony?
- When was a time when you felt God the most?
- What is your testimony?

JOURNALING AND PRAYERS

CHAPTER TEN

Visualization

As I have said, I am a part of my high school's worship team. While at worship, I was having an extremely difficult time singing loudly. To help me, someone suggested visualizing the space and trying to sing to reach something that was far away. I tried to visualize a tree that was on the other side of a long field; when I did this, my singing was more fluid and easier. I went home and practiced and practiced and practiced. I finally mastered the skill of singing loudly. At school while we were prepping for the worship service, I did better than I had the previous day. Once I finally was ready, the songs that we were going to sing got cut out of the chapel service. I was disappointed, but I was glad that I had gotten the practice in.

When we go through life, sometimes we have an exact idea of what our future looks like. When we do this, God can be left out of the equation. This can be dangerous. I am guilty of it, and there are probably others who are too. When we have an idea of what we want our future to look like, God might have a very different idea than that. That is why we need to not visualize what we want our future to look like; we need to imagine what God wants our world to look like.

Another example of visualization goes into writing. In writing, the best way to set up a scene is to describe everything so precisely that the reader knows things that haven't actually been said. So my proposal is this: As Christians, are we acting like a descriptive essay? Are we letting other people know that we are Christians without actually saying it? We should be a reflection of Jesus and others should see Jesus in our hearts as we live every day. Is there enough evidence to convict you of being a Christian? I hope that there is for me and for you. One pet peeve of mine is being "fake." You probably know what I mean. Those people who call themselves Christians and act like they love God at church, but then when the week starts, they are the total opposite. No one is perfect, but are we total opposites when it comes to church versus our weekdays? I want someone to look at me and not see me but see a woman on the fire for the Lord, a woman who has the Holy Spirit burning within her.

There are many people who label themselves Christians, but how many of us are living out the truth?

Chapter 10 Reflection

- Have you ever visualized something?
- Is there enough evidence to convict you of being a Christian?
- Are you letting God "set the scenery" for your future?
- Do you act the same in your faith at different places, or are you different at church than you are at work?

JOURNALING AND PRAYERS

CHAPTER ELEVEN

Calm in the Storm

Whether storms are mental or literal, they are almost never associated with happiness or peace. Hurricane Sandy, Hurricane Katrina, tsunamis—destruction and despair. Mental storms can include terrible thoughts, depression, stress, anxiety—the list goes on and on. Through all the storms that we are trying to get through, we try to seek God. At our most weak points, this is when we seek God. For some, it is the opposite, only seeking God when our lives seem perfect. But have you ever thought about praising God both in the storm and in the silence? In scriptures, we find God both in the calm and in the storm.

"The LORD said, 'Go out and stand on the mountain in the presence of the LORD, for the LORD is about to pass by.' Then a great and powerful wind tore the mountains apart and shattered the rocks before the LORD, but the LORD was not in the wind. After the wind there was an earthquake, but the LORD was not in the earthquake. After the earthquake came a fire, but the LORD was not in the fire. And after the fire came a gentle whisper. When Elijah heard it, he pulled his cloak over his face and went out and stood at the mouth of the cave. Then a voice said to him, 'What are you doing here, Elijah?'" (1 Kings 19:11–13 NIV)

This passage demonstrates God in the calm. Elijah was so focused on finding God that all the storms were distractions when God was right in front of him. Sometimes, we forget to take a break and to make time for God to speak to us while it is quiet. With all the noise on this earth, it can be hard to concentrate on the voice that matters. We had a sermon about this very topic, and it posed this question, "Does God's voice interest you the most?" Why are we seeking opinions that don't matter when we could be seeking God's? Personally, I need to make time to talk to God one-on-one. Even if I have a thousand things going on at once, it actually relieves stress to bring my problems up to God. I have learned to make God's voice the one that counts. It can be hard to hear His gentle whisper through the things that I face through the day, but I am reassured by that whisper.

I was in prayer group at my school, and someone said something about the calm in a storm. This was ironic to me because there had just been an album that came out with almost the same title that I had been listening to.

For the rest of that week, I kept hearing that phrase. I think that God tries to show us that He is everywhere, not only in the big things, but also in the small ones that He longs for us to recognize.

The storm part of this concept reminds me of this series of verses:

"Immediately Jesus made the disciples get into the boat and go on ahead of Him to the other side, while He dismissed the crowd. After He had dismissed them, He went up on a mountainside by Himself to pray. Later that night, He was there alone, and the boat was already a considerable distance from land, buffeted by the waves because the wind was against it. Shortly before dawn Jesus went out to them, walking on the lake. When the disciples saw Him walking on the lake, they were terrified. 'It's a ghost,' they said, and cried out in fear. But Jesus immediately said to them: 'Take courage! It is I. Don't be afraid.'

'Lord, if it's you,' Peter replied, 'tell me to come to you on the water.' 'Come,' He said. Then Peter got down out of the boat, walked on the water and came toward Jesus. But when he saw the wind, he was afraid and, beginning to sink, cried out, 'Lord, save me!' Immediately Jesus reached out His hand and caught him. 'You of little faith,' he said, 'why did you doubt?' And when they climbed into the boat, the wind died down. Then those who were in the boat worshiped Him, saying, 'Truly you are the Son of God.'" (Matthew 14:22–33)

When we are in a storm, we can start doubting God in the midst of it. When we do this, we start to sink while Jesus is holding out His hand for us to take. God is in the storm and calls us into the unknown where He is. He wants us to walk on the water and trust in Him.

The eye of the hurricane is said to be the most peaceful. While chaos and anarchy is all around, the center is filled with peace and stillness.

Applying this, God calls us to the center of our worries, where He gives us peace and fulfills us. We just need to get through the destructive layer to reach the peace in the center of it all.

Jesus will not sleep when we need Him. Often we think of Him to be somewhere far away on a hillside or up in the clouds, but He will come to us in the middle of every trial we face. Whether we go to prison, the hospital, a third world country, or even in a storm, God will meet us where we are.

Jesus walked the walk with us and continued to stay by our sides through everything.

We have a choice; do not praise God, praise God in the calm, praise God in the storm, or praise God in everything. What is your choice?

"Be strong and courageous. Do not be afraid or terrified because of them, for the Lord your God goes with you; He will never leave you nor forsake you." (Deuteronomy 31:6 NIV)

I think back to the tornado in Oklahoma. That one event altered so many lives in negative ways but also in very impactful and positive ways. You may wonder how something so horrific could bring positivity into light, but there is a way. Many were baptized after the event and came to know Christ because of the safety that He provided for their families.

Is God trying to speak to you through a struggle? You may feel weak and hopeless, but through everything that is happening, God has a will and a perfect plan for your life, so please, do not be afraid. The Bible says the phrase "Do not be afraid" around 115 times in the NIV. There is a reason for this. God doesn't want us to worry and He makes that very clear to us. God holds our future in His hands, and He longs for the best outcome in our lives, so there is no need to worry because God has it under control.

"Therefore, since we have been justified through faith, we have peace with God through our Lord Jesus Christ, through whom we have gained access by faith into this grace in which we now stand. And we boast in the hope of the glory of God. Not only so, but we also glory in our sufferings, because we know that suffering produces perseverance; perseverance, character; and character, hope." (Romans 5:1–4 NIV)

God will keep you safe through your storm, He will provide hope out of our suffering because He is the Lord. Jesus provided hope through His suffering on the cross, and God will help us develop hope out of our misery the same way He delivered hope out of Jesus.

Hope is the anchor for our soul. My favorite Bible verse declares this exact thing.

"We have this hope as an anchor for the soul, firm and secure." (Hebrews 6:19 NIV)

I love that piece of scripture because it cuts straight to the point. The hope that God gives us is a precious gift that He gave to us. The cross is a symbol of hope—Jesus is a symbol of hope, and there is hope around us every day. We all have fallen short of the glory of God, but with Jesus, we have hope of eternal life because of what Jesus did for us on the cross. He was the only sinless human that ever inhabited the earth. Either we were destined to die or He was destined to die to save all of us. Jesus came to serve and to provide hope for every sinner so that we can spend eternity with the one we belong with. We do not belong to the world. If the world hates us and everyone seems like they're against us every step of the way, it's because we don't belong to the world. God welcomes us and protects us, so we can have the confidence that we belong to Him. So through the hope that Jesus gave us, we can live with our Father, the one that we are meant to be with.

Have you ever felt like you were in a place where you could not possibly fix what you've done? This is the context in Romans 5: Paul wanted the followers in Rome to understand that they could not fix what they had done. He did this to give them a greater appreciation of what amazing gift that God had blessed them with. Through our lives, we come across many things that we wish to restore and redeem, but the truth is that we can't. This is what Paul wanted the Christians to understand. He wanted them to know that there was something that separated us from God that was unable to be redeemed, sin. Though this seems extremely negative, there is an extreme plus side. God has done what we cannot do ourselves. Going back to the same verses from earlier, Romans 5:1–4, we can see these exact things. The root of the word "justify" or "justice" goes back to a measuring reed or tool. It was a measuring standard that we cannot measure up to. To solve this problem, God sent Jesus Christ to the cross. Jesus, a young man and God's only son, took the yoke of our sins upon Him and suffered the most excruciating death upon His body physically, mentally, and spiritually.

Because God did this, we have all been pardoned of our sin and made just. The word "faith" is so important for us to understand. It means to put weight upon something. The only way you will know if something will hold you is if you put your faith into it. For example, if you were to sit in a chair, how can you be sure that it will hold you? The only exact way to know this is by sitting in it or putting your faith/weight into it. So when we bind ourselves with Jesus Christ, we are made pure and sinless. Paul tells the Romans that because we have been made just with God, we are also at peace with Him. This peace is not a subjective, emotional thing. This peace is a state of being. Even as children, as innocent as we looked, we were all born into a hostile relationship with God. Now that we have placed our full trust into Jesus, we have the state of being peaceful. Now, the war has ended, and there is no hostility in our relationship between us and God. Some picture God to be holding a gavel in His hand, but that is not the case. There isn't condemnation for anyone who is in Christ. Much like fights that have been victorious throughout history, there is celebration afterward. So why don't we celebrate? Just because the war is over in our life and we are at peace with God does not mean that there isn't a war breaking out around us.

There's war all around us. Starving families, broken relationships—just because we are at peace with God does not mean that the world is or our neighbors are. Paul was trying to get this message across. We did not earn salvation; we received it from God. The only contribution that we participated in was putting our weight on Jesus. Even then, God has brought us into this relationship, and we have peace. Paul says because of this, one day, there will be no suffering, pain, sorrows, depression, or any negativity, because one day, Jesus is coming back. When Jesus comes back, He will make all things right. Everything will be restored and fixed. He will make what we long to see fixed right. Paul says that the desire to go and be with Jesus should fill our hearts. The day is coming that no negativity will exist, so we need to fix our eyes on hope. We long for heaven to come because we want things to be made right. Knowing this, that hope we have should be motivating us to proclaim the amazing news that Jesus gave and demonstrate the gospel so that anyone that does not have a peace with God can be met. They can gain the knowledge about who Jesus is and discover that if they place their faith in Jesus, they will have the opportunity to dwell with God forever in peace because of what Jesus has done for them.

We are eager for Jesus to come back, and many times, we might get impatient. God has a purpose for the wait. He knows that there are many people who have not learned about the news of what Jesus gave to them. If Jesus were to come this very moment, there would still be a large amount of people who have not accepted God and would not be ready for His return.

The goal as Christians should be to spread the word of God to as many people we can in the shortest possible amount of time. Sometimes, we can be selfish because we are only thinking that our relationship with God matters, but all other relationships with Him do too.

In all fairness, I think that our society is very narcissistic in its time. If you think about it, many things that we tend to do during the day revolve around us. Some examples include selfies, social media in general, and sometimes even in prayer. I am guilty of doing what some call the "grocery list" prayer. This is when you have a list of things that you want or expect from God to deliver, but you are so caught up in what you want that you don't focus on what God wants for you. Not only individuals focus on themselves, but some groups are very self-centered. Christianity has branched out into many different denominations. For example, there is even a denomination with four people in its village within my state. (We recently went to the Canterbury Shaker Village in New Hampshire for a field trip). (This picture is taken from the Shaker Village)

My school welcomes all denominations of Christianity, which I think is the correct response for what Christians are called to do. If there were not denominations of Christianity, imagine how much easier it would be to agree on the main point of our faith. God loves us and sent His son to die for our sins. I think that we can become so focused on our own denomination that we become narcissistic in our faith. We welcome some people into our faith and push others away. This is not what we are supposed to do! God calls us to be welcoming and loving of everyone. After all, isn't this what God did for us?

"Accept one another, then, just as Christ accepted you, in order to bring praise to God." (Romans 15:7 NIV)

It really is as simple as that; we need to welcome all and love them like Jesus did.

Chapter 11 Reflection

- Where are you looking for God?
- Do you allow God to speak to you in the silence and in the distraction?
- Have you accepted the gift of hope that God blessed us with?
- How can you accept everyone?

JOURNALING AND PRAYERS

CHAPTER TWELVE

Miracles

A baby opens its eyes for the first time, and the mother embraces her child. A sick man is healed after carrying a terminal ailment, and two missionaries are rescued after being held for ransom. Do you believe in miracles?

Miracles can be something small or something that seemed impossible turned into something extremely possible. Miracles, along with prophecy, are two things that shape the word of God into the infallible truth that it is.

Prophecy is something that is so specific that there is no possible way that a man could simply come up with it. God planned all these things for a very specific purpose.

Just like the miracles and prophecy that God has implanted into His word, God places very specific things into our lives at the perfect time. Here are a few examples.

My mom and brother were having some strain in their relationship. My mom was very upset and prayed for God to show her a sign that He heard her prayer. My brother and mom were in the car and went to a store of some sort. In the parking lot, a woman walked up to my mother and offered to pray with her. She told my mom that she felt like she needed to pray for my brother and her. This was a sign that God had heard my mother's prayer.

A similar story in the Bible was when Hagar took her son into the desert. She needed to hear the Lord to help her and her son, but she didn't think that there was any hope left. God talked to her in her weakness, and Hagar named her son Ishmael because "God hears."

Another example of God placing things in our lives at the right moments is very simple. Have you ever seen the same Bible verse or message appear throughout your week or day? I remember a verse in Colossians kept appearing in my life. This helped me to write parts of this manuscript, and it also allowed God to speak to me through scripture.

I never understood how God could "speak" to us. I used to hear many adults say that God told them to do something, but I was very confused because God never physically spoke to me. But as I grew with age, I realized that God speaks to us through scripture, and through other people. It would be very easy to push aside our doubts if God physically talked to us on a regular basis, but every time I think of that, I also think of this verse:

"Then Jesus told him, 'Because you have seen me, you have believed; blessed are those who have not seen and yet have believed.'" (John 20:29 NIV)

I know that it can be hard to speak to God without an audible response, but I think that this makes our relationship with God even stronger than it originally was. If we spend time with our creator and cannot see Him now, just imagine what our relationship with God will be like when we get to spend forever by His side.

In a class that I take, we spend time to discuss tough questions that we have. One week, we were talking about how our relationships should show God through us. So if we build our relationship with God on the truth, then we can outwardly show others how we live. The question that week was "How do we love another person if there is mutual hatred between us?" At first, I deemed this question as difficult, but with research and discussion, this question was easily answered. My answer was this, You can only change how you live and show other people. So if a particular person despises you, but you also despise them, you can alter the way that you act toward them so that the hostility would dissolve. God calls us to love our enemies, and if we are against the idea, we should realize that love is what defeats hatred.

"You have heard that it was said, 'Love your neighbor and hate your enemy.' But I tell you, love your enemies and pray for those who persecute you, that you may be the children of your father in heaven." (Matthew 5:43–44 NIV)

So if we want to be rebellious anyway, why shouldn't we be rebellious in love? If the world wants us to hate each other, let's love one another!

After all, we do not belong to this world. The verse of the week at school is this:

"'If the world hates you, keep in mind that it hated me first. If you belonged to the world, it would love you as its own. As it is, you do not belong to the world, but I have chosen you out of the world. That is why the world hates you.'" (John 15:18–19 NIV)

So if we don't belong to this world, just imagine how amazing our world will be. My pastor proposed this to us: if God created the earth in the short amount of time that He did, imagine what heaven looks like since there has been so much time.

Chapter 12 Reflection

- Do you believe in miracles?
- What miracles are in your life?
- How has God spoken to you through a miracle?

JOURNALING AND PRAYERS

CHAPTER THIRTEEN

Mission

I sit in a comfy blue chair on the third floor of my school. The room is empty, but I can hear the laughter of my peers. The sunlight seeps in through the window at a perfect angle that warms me as I await dismissal. This final chapter is to get straight to the point, and tell you that life is what you make it. For a while, I was struggling to write this book because I was so stressed out and a lot was going on around me. I was so focused on all the obstacles that were overcoming me that I didn't once thank God for how amazing my life is. No one has a perfect life, but what we put in is what we get out. Find the little things, and be grateful for what this world does have to offer. Even the simple things can offer happiness, there is just an effort that needs to be put in so that we can find the blessing in our lives.

To sum up this book, I would say this: God loves you so much, and you have a purpose to glorify Him through all that you do. Through all the struggles that you go through, know that God will get you through all of it. He created everything in this world, and He knows more about you than you do yourself. Be grateful, and listen to God's voice over all the others. God gave us the opportunity to love on others so that there will be more people in the kingdom of heaven. Our mission on this earth is heaven-sent.

JOURNALING AND PRAYERS

"Impact"

This final section is here for you to write your thoughts after reading this book, or how it may have made an impact on you. Feel free to write or draw anything that comes to mind.

ABOUT THE AUTHOR

Emma Beauchesne, a teen with New England roots, was born and raised in New Hampshire and lived in Florida for some time as well. Though young, she is driven and always looking for something new to add to her list of hobbies. She is an avid scuba diver and has traveled to Belize, Little Cayman, Canada, and the Dominican Republic. Her highest educational accomplishments include three honors classes and a college course through MITX in Python programming completed in 2015. She continues to challenge herself with a course through UQX. Her dream to become a Christian recording artist and her love of Christian music led her to sing on her school worship team. In addition, she is a self-taught acoustic guitarist and has experience playing the electric bass guitar. She has been active in track, cross-country, and basketball. She has always loved writing and is supported by her family, teachers, and peers in her pursuit of writing. Emma lives with her parents; Jason and Jennifer, her brother; Jack, and her sweet orange tabby cat; Fifi. Most importantly, Emma has a heart for the Lord. Her relationship with God is something she longs to share with others, and has a heck of a fun time doing it.